SHARING THE MEDICINE OF LOVE

BY

VAL COOK

JILL LITTLE, PHD.

ISBN 978-0-61564-477-6
(Volume 1)

For those who wish to contact the authors or order
SHARING THE MEDICINE OF LOVE,
please contact
CookandLittle@aol.com
Educational discounts are available

CONTENTS

IT IS TIME TO CHANGE

Our achievements are spectacular. Our intellectual acumen produced industry befitting an intellectually based society. Our Spiritual barrenness has resulted in self destruction, egoic warring and moral abandonment. It is time to change.

Asleep for generations, God whispers to us: it is time. Set aside the plow, the plane, the prejudice, the chaos. Awaken your purpose. Unfold your love without fear of mockery and abandon. It is time to change.

Jill Little
Awakened By the Light

CHAPTER 1

THE BEGINNING

I could see the headlines now, "HUSBAND SLASHES WIFE'S THROAT, KILLS BABY!" What could three women do to help console this cousin of ours who lost her only child and nearly died herself at the hands of her husband? It was such an incredible tragedy.

I drove silently down the country road, working our way to Oka, Quebec. My mother and my Aunt Tillie were silent on the outside, but I knew our thoughts were all fighting to understand how this could ever happen. We have had catastrophes in our family but this was clearly the most cataclysmic and the most heartbreaking.

We were happy to arrive at Thomas's house. It was a long drive from Onondaga Nation. It was an early July morning. The air was heavy, like our shoulders, as we started walking towards my cousin's house. We noticed a few vehicles were there already. I hadn't seen Thomas or his family in years; now I was here to ask his permission to hold a small 'gathering of love' ceremony for his daughter. I knew this was the right thing to do but I kept reassuring myself over and over to be brave and fearless. It was hard to be strong, but I had the two strongest people I know at my side. We had love and positive energy on our side. We were determined that, while this was different from our first ceremony, our intentions were the same. I can't believe it was two years ago when we started it all.

Being the observer that I have become, I had realized how little time was set aside for the 'celebration' of a girl to womanhood (menstruation). We native women prefer to call it our 'Moontime.' Without going into too much detail, we believe we are governed by Grandmother Moon which enables us to be vessels of life. Our attitude is that 'Moontime' is a great gift and not a burden every month; it should lift a young girl's head up high with self-respect and pride, knowing the magic she carries for humankind within her.

With that said, I had decided many years ago to have some sort of celebration for my grandchildren when it was their time. As it turned out, it was my son's daughter, Karen that was the first honoree.

It was perhaps a little clumsy. God knows I was nervous and wanted it to be so perfect. I asked my husband of his thoughts and he gave me nothing but encouragement. "Val", he said, "anything positive has no wrong way; just do it."

I asked my medicine man, who happens to be my brother, Jerome, if he had any advice for the ceremony. He had some good ideas and I incorporated them into my ceremony. He told me always to make sure I asked permission, whether it be from the girl, from the mother of the girl, and/or from the grandmother, mainly because, as natives, we are ruled by our Matrilineal Society of the clan system.

In our society, a child is seen as a precious gift, embraced into a life of family, a clan, and ultimately a nation. We teach the children the traditions of our native community. They must learn their history. For example, I come from my mother who is of the Wolf Clan. I cannot marry another Wolf because that would be like marrying my brother. My husband was of the Eel Clan, as was his mother. The elders watch closely and set things right if a relative is attracted to another of the same clan. Bloodline has something to do with it as well. We would not marry a cousin even if they were of a different clan.

My father's mother was from the Snipe Clan. She would always remind us that if you can remember a relative, no matter how far removed, it's still too close to marry.

So it happened, by the time I was ready to make this dream of mine a reality, it was my third granddaughter that I honored. Karen is my son's oldest daughter. She is of the Turtle Clan and at the time of her ceremony, she was twelve years old.

Before I called Karen's mother, I thought carefully about what I would say. She was absolutely delighted to have her daughter be the first of what would be an incredible tradition. I made her aware of my intentions to invite many relatives.

Each person I called was asked to bring a small gift for Karen, so that each time she looked at the gift, she would recall her celebration. Along with these gifts, each would be asked to give their thoughts of love, wisdom and encouragement. I personally had been searching for the right words to say for many years. I wanted it to be perfect in every way. This was my purpose, which still fills me with great excitement and satisfaction.

The ceremony asked that everyone make personal contact with Karen by gently washing her from her head to her arms and hands and finally her feet, with a basin of cedar water prepared earlier in the day. The washing is symbolic of washing away childhood and rejoicing in her new found womanhood.

Although I do not speak our native language, I believe the Creator knows my intentions and hears my prayers of thanks to both He and to the medicine of the cedar tree being used for this ceremony. This is a long held tradition that is important in my family.

Since the cedar water is considered medicine, we set the celebration for ten in the morning, and, as native, we like to do medicine before noon. We were all assembled in my living room. With respect for this personal ceremony, my husband left for the day. It took perhaps less than an hour but it was the most moving sixty minutes we could ever hope to share.

In our beliefs, we start any ceremony from right to left when we gather or meet. Consequently, Karen was seated on a wooden chair as we sat facing her in a semi-circle. I made sure I put a simple plastic tablecloth on the floor under her chair since I didn't know how wet it might become with the basin of cedar water.

Karen was very nervous, and at times, silly. Everyone else was full of high energy and engaging as we greeted each new arrival. We see each other often at picnics and dinners, but this was different. It was a Moontime ceremony, the beginning of a tradition. This was new to us all; excitement was the order of the day. I loved it.

When everyone had settled down, I began speaking of what we were here for: to give Karen our love and our positive words. They all knew what was expected as they took their seats. My beautiful daughter, Isa, started the ceremony first because she was the first to Karen's right. I was so proud of how she softly caressed Karen's face, washing lightly as she stroked downward, all the while telling her of her love for Karen. Reinforcing her lineage, Isa reminded her that, although they were not of the same clan, they were of the same blood and she would forever be her Auntie. What beautiful words she spoke that day. Isa gave Karen a handmade set of beaded barrettes to help complete her native outfit.

Isa's two teenage daughters each took their turn, not without some awkward laughter as they were unsure of what to say. But when each got into the moment, they said some powerful words of kinship and love that I know will be with Karen forever.

My sister, Sandy and her adult daughter, Susan were actually quite thrilled about the Moontime ceremony. They, of course, did not know Karen as well as my girls did, but they had loving words for her. They offered their respect and gave encouragement to her in her new status of womanhood. They let Karen know how lucky she was to have such a ceremony. They gave her thoughtful gifts, including a journal to write her memories of this day. I was so proud and grateful to them for attending, despite their busy lives.

Karen's mother had been sitting quietly in the corner of the sectional couch, nervous but observant, really not saying much of anything. She walked up to her daughter, wetted the wash cloth and began washing her baby girl, her first born, now realizing that, inevitably, her daughter was a young woman. We all had tears flowing down our cheeks, tears of love.

My daughter, Lori, was next. It amazed me how she really came into her own while talking to her niece. She offered her a listening ear, at any time, day or night, and made it clear that she meant it. Karen may not have realized what her aunt was offering, but perhaps in the future, when the tides of emotion throw Karen into turmoil during her Moontime, she will remember to call her Auntie or pay her a visit. What a significant, deeply thoughtful offer. My body fills again with pride when I remember this.

Finally it was my turn. I knew what I wanted to say. After all, I had spent years waiting for this moment. I reviewed everything in my mind: how I wanted to remind Karen of her family ties, keeping respect for her and others, being responsible to her family, clan, community and nation. I then pushed myself out of the recliner and picked up the washcloth. "It's my turn, finally…"

I just barely got it out, "I love you and I've waited all these years and this is the moment……….." I began to cry. My heart was filled with so much happiness and gratefulness to all for helping me accomplish this moment. It was just overwhelming. Wouldn't you know that everyone else burst into tears as well? I brought out the Pendleton blanket that I had purchased for Karen, only because it had a Turtle on it. That is her clan.

I then invited everyone to come up and empower it with their love and strength. I wrapped it around her and everyone hugged and kissed Karen. I then told her that should she experience a difficult time in her life to come, she should wrap herself in the blanket and be comforted and loved in the memory of our "Moontime" celebration. She will always find us in her time of need. We held each other tightly, bonding our lives forever.

After everyone recovered from the emotionally-filled ritual, I served a strawberry drink and half-moon cookies to one and all. The symbolism of the menu was obvious.

My husband, Ed, my brother, Jerome and especially my son, Lewis were greatly supportive and proud of me for creating this event. It lifts my spirit to know that.

CHAPTER 2

STARTING A NEW TRADITION

Val and I were visiting, as old friends do, one afternoon in the middle of summer. We sat by the lake, taking in the warmth of the day. Val is a dear friend; younger in years but amazingly wise. She is a Native American, which I believe has much to do with her enormous ability to observe people and understand their situations in life. She has fabulous dreams, some of which could become movies, really. This July day we were catching each other up on our grandchildren; how they were growing; their life problems and promises; the usual grandmother talk. But Val caught my attention when she told me of a ceremony she had initiated with her granddaughter, who had recently gone into her 'Moontime'. (That would be her first menstrual cycle, for those of us non-natives). I was fascinated to hear all about it, especially because Val is the ultimate storyteller.

Not surprisingly, the ceremony was very spiritual. Val had given every aspect a great deal of consideration. She wanted everyone who participated to have a deeply moving experience.

She told me she had gone to the woods to gather a cedar branch. She had asked permission of the tree to take it, and then left her tobacco as a thank you for the gift. Val also asked permission of her daughter-in-law to have a ceremony for her granddaughter. She told me her daughter-in-law was excited to have it happen, knowing well that her mother-in-law was a woman of great love.

Val told me how beautiful the ceremony was and how emotionally moving it became for everyone in the room. She said that everyone there was crying with tears of love and joy for the special moment. At the end of the ceremony she used a blanket that she wrapped around her beloved granddaughter. I was so moved, listening to the beauty of it all.

After wiping away my tears of appreciation, I asked Val if she thought I could do this with my granddaughter, Sally. She had reached her Moontime and I was thrilled at the prospect of honoring her life with this special moment.

Val, in her inimitable, loving way, turned to me with a big hug and said, "Of course you can do this, honey! You don't have to be a native. We laughed.

Then I told her I was nervous about it. I didn't have the confidence that Val had with such things. She'd been doing ceremonies all her life. What if I screwed it up? Or embarrassed Sally? Or embarrassed us both?

Val looked me square in the eyes and said, "Jill, there's no right or wrong way to the ceremony! All you have to do is have love in your heart for her, and we both know you're over flowing with it." That's all I needed. I knew Val was on to something great. It was going to be great for Sally, and it would be great for so many other people I could think of who needed affirmation of their worth and purpose in this world.

Val and I talked and talked. There were so many possibilities beyond 'Moontime' celebrations. Our heads were swimming in ideas. We knew there was more to this ceremony that was yet to be uncovered. Val had been inspired with an idea that could change hearts from sadness to joy. This ritual could also help so many who are full of fear, loss and tragedy in their lives. It was then that we decided to write a book to recruit an army of love celebrators who would be willing to open their hearts, unconditionally, and without judgment. We would put it in God's hands for the help we needed to make this happen.

It was Labor Day weekend. Our first born grandchild, Sally, had arrived two days early to spend 'alone' time with my husband and I. Each year we plan all the special things we want to do together. The usual routine is to go out for dinner the day after her arrival. Then the next day we go to the New York State Fair. We've always been lucky with the weather. Rain can be a pain in the neck because everyone on the midway rushes to the buildings for cover; the crowds can be stifling.

Our first stop after the entry gate is to make our way down the street to the dairy building to see the butter sculpture and then drink the long anticipated twenty–five cent glass of chocolate milk, made by the local dairies. It's always so cold and delicious; a far cry from my usual skim milk. From there its sampling cheese, maple candy, and baked potatoes filled with every imaginable combination of sour cream, chives, butter and bacon. It's an "eating experience," as Sally lovingly describes it. From there it's countless animal building, filled with the noise of crowing chickens, thumping bunnies, and squealing children. We feel the freshly shorn sheep, new born calves and anything else we can experience. It's a comforting routine that Sally, Ed (my husband) and I have grown to love and enjoy. This year she started asking for the midway, with its games and rides. This year we knew she was starting to grow up.

Our daughter, Sarah, Sally's mother, arrived with the rest of her family the day before Labor Day. The only one missing was her ex-husband, which was hard on us all. Sarah felt like a duck out of water after fifteen years of marriage and having him at her side. The children struggled with the awkwardness of loving two people who decided that their marriage needed to end, and they had no choice but to accept the aftermath of it all.

I was anxious to speak privately with Sarah about the special ceremony Val had celebrated with her granddaughter. I had no doubt that Sarah would be open to having Sally honored in this way; Sarah is a very spiritual, loving woman. But it was important that I ask her permission because she is Sally's mother. It would be presumptuous of me to bypass Sarah's wishes in this matter, and disrespectful as well.

Sarah seemed pleased at the prospect of Sally's Moontime ceremony, so I spoke to Sally privately to see if she was willing to have a special moment with me before she went to bed. She seemed puzzled but told me she was fine with whatever. She would shower, put on her pajamas and meet me in my bedroom.

As I lit the candles and prepared the special quilt I had for her, I asked God to help me speak the right words to my beautiful granddaughter. I wasn't Val. I had never experienced any ceremonies in my youth, other than sorority stuff, which was hardly the same. I looked at the quilt, lying on the floor beside the spot where I planned to sit beside Sally. Funny, I thought. I had bought this quilt in an old barn in Maine two years ago. It was from the 1800's. I marveled at the hand work and wondered how many stories were told while this beautiful piece of art was being made. Now I knew why I had bought it. I also knew why I somehow had never used it.

I sat alone, waiting for Sally. She was in my bathroom, humming away. I was feeling anxious. I wanted this to be so perfect for my special little granddaughter. She was becoming a woman before my eyes. I had briefly considered having Sarah there, but decided I was too much a novice at this and I didn't want to make it more complicated. I only had primitive instincts working for me, and truthfully, I was afraid I'd mess it all up. It was so important to me that this moment be special enough that Sally would carry it in her heart forever. I have so much love and respect for her, and I knew she deserved to hear about how much her life means to me.

Sally appeared in the doorway, all shiny from her shower; her hair still wet. She was the image of purity. I knew she was excited and full of anticipation. Her eyes smiled at me and I knew we would both be okay.

She sat on the floor, cross-legged and anxious to understand the significance of what was happening. I moved the quilt next to her and began my words of love. I wish I could repeat all that I said, but it wasn't recorded. It was straight from my heart. I held her hand and I told Sally how I remembered going to Rochester the day she was born. Of sitting with her mom until it was close to her delivery; of walking the streets and worrying about my own little girl, Sarah; wishing for a speedy labor; hoping her body wouldn't be in jeopardy; praying that her child would be strong and healthy; knowing all these things were in God's hands.

Sally looked into my eyes warmly relishing the story of her birth. I told her how tiny she was; of counting all her toes and fingers. She was red and wrinkly and beautiful.

The stories spun about her toddler years; what she may or may not have remembered of the joyful moments I could recall. How she was so very, very special; that there was nobody like her on this earth. Sally was a unique soul who is here on earth to complete her part in God's work.

Sally looked peaceful. She seemed to understand that the world needed her. She understood that the talents she was acquiring would be useful in her life's purpose.

I don't know how long we were together. At some point I put the quilt around Sally and told her that I would always love her and be there for her. I told her that she was now becoming a woman; it was time to put childish things behind her. She should, however, always keep the innocence that she has in all that she does; most importantly, she needed to love with all her heart and soul, because loving is the most important thing in life.

I was in full crying mode by now, wiping my nose and blubbering about how I hoped Sally would always put the quilt around her when she was sad and to put the quilt around her when she was happy, and that my love would be there, too.

We hugged for a long time. It was wonderful for me, and I believe it was for her, too. What was really great is that when I visited her several weeks later, I went upstairs to her bedroom and there it was – her Moontime quilt at the bottom of her bed. My tears rose again, and I knew that Sally remembered.

The only thing I didn't tell Sally, and I will the next time I see her, is to use the quilt as a sign to her mother or me (or her father for that matter) when she has something extremely important to discuss and full attention and understanding are needed for her. All she needs to do is put the quilt under her arm and say "I need to talk to you." This will be a tool for her lifetime that opens the doors of communication so that she will never feel alone in an impossible situation. That is the beauty of the quilt and this ceremony.

CHAPTER 3

HONORING HER

My daughter-in –law was having a celebration for her 40th birthday. She invited about forty of her girlfriends and, happily, me too. We have a great relationship. She is very open with me, and I with her. Sometimes I overstep my place in giving opinions on issues concerning her beautiful children but she forgives me for it, knowing how much I love them, and tells me when she doesn't want to "hear it." We respect each other. I love her like a daughter.

Val and I were talking on the phone and I asked her what she thought of using the "Moon time" ceremony for a birthday celebration at Lilly's party. Val was quiet at first and then said, "Why not? You love her. You want to honor her!"

We discussed the two ceremonies, and found there was more similarity of intent then differences between them. I told her I wasn't sure yet about doing it. My plan was to take the beautiful white silk comforter that I had bought in Florida and, interestingly, had used only to cover her children on one occasion for a special story time in my bedroom. I would leave it in the car and make a decision after I mulled around with Lilly's friends.

My doubts were not about performing the ceremony, but about the fact that I didn't know how most of these young women would react to it. I didn't want to make anyone uncomfortable. It is a very emotional, even draining, experience because so much love is evoked. Also, I didn't want to somehow embarrass Lilly. Having a mother-in-law expressing her love for you at a social gathering could be over the top for many people.

As I tucked the comforter in the back seat of my car, I remember thinking that it may very well be resting there upon my return home. As I drove down the road I pictured different scenarios for honoring Lilly; I wondered if it was just too ambitious an undertaking. I was really nervous about making the right decision. I decided it was going to have to be a last minute call.

The birthday party was brimming with beautiful thirty and forty-somethings. One was more lovely and bubbly than the next. These women were happy to be alive and showed it. I gratefully noticed two gals whom I had previously met and incidentally were nearer my age. We chatted about how lovely Lilly and Scott's new home was, and how beautiful the dining room looked with all the sparkling china. The food looked delicious; I remember how hungry I was.

When I saw Sharon, I was excited for Lilly. Sharon had come all the way from New Jersey for the party. She is a childhood friend and they've kept in touch over the years. They shared many memories over the years. She had been there for Lilly's heartache when, at the age of ten, her mother passed away with cancer. She had been there for her joy as well, having been her maid of honor, and now tonight for her 'big' birthday.

After we hugged, I asked Sharon what she thought of my idea to celebrate Lilly's birthday. Her eyes answered   before she did. She grabbed my hands; her eyes filled with tears, and said, "I can't believe this. I was thinking of honoring her in some way, but I just couldn't figure it out. This is perfect! But do you mind if I say some words to Lilly, too?"
"Of course! Absolutely!" I couldn't get the words out fast enough. What a perfect idea. I told Sharon that it would be fabulous to have her participate, too. In fact, why not invite some of Lilly's other friends join in! What a celebration this would be!

The evening air chilled the patio dwellers; a few at a time came into the house. Lilly announced that it was time to eat. The girl's lined up around the beautifully adorned table; Lilly had her best china for the special occasion. Then they disappeared into other rooms to find chairs and flat spaces to dine with each other.

It was exciting for me: the prospect of honoring Lilly. What made it even more spectacular was the enthusiasm that greeted me as I told each of her "close" friends about the celebration. They wanted to be a part of it all. I slipped out the door to retrieve the silk comforter that waited in my back seat. I decided to tuck it behind the family room sofa for now.

The time for birthday cake arrived, with everyone trying to fit into the dining room. Lilly thanked everyone profusely for coming to her party. She thanked her friend Sharon, especially for making such an effort to drive so far; then a neighbor who had become a dear friend, who had helped her so much during her move. Then, to my incredible surprise, she turned to me. She told everyone that I was her mother-in-law but she really thought of me as her mother. I chocked back the tears that welled in my eyes. I gave her a huge hug. It was a heart-felt moment for me to be acknowledged as such an important person in Lilly's life.

It was true; Lilly and I are very close. The loss of her mother to cancer had been life changing for her. When she married into our family she was slow to completely accept our love. She had long held barriers that kept her heart in a safe place. Now I believe that she realizes that we truly love her as part of our family.

The cake was frosted like a wedding cake, and absolutely

delicious. We finished eating and went to the sofa. She sat next to me, asking if I was enjoying myself. She is like that; very aware and sensitive to her friends and family. I hugged her again, thanking her for including me. I caught Sharon's eye and signaled her to funnel the guests into the room. I asked Lilly to stay on the couch as I got up to fetch the quilt. She looked at me quizzically. She was trying to figure out what was happening.

With my teacher voice I asked the young women to quiet down for a moment. As they did, I placed the quilt behind and around Lilly. It was very large and actually looked awkward, but the fabric was perfect for her. Her eyes began to fill because she knew of the ceremony I had done with Sally. She knew this was going to be about honoring her now.

Though the words aren't entirely in the same order, I remember vividly the approximate introduction.

"Ladies, as you may remember, I'm Lilly's mother-in-law. I'm here to celebrate her life with you. She is so special to me. I love her with all my heart. I love her especially because she has brought such joy to my son. And because she is such a loving mother to her sons." It was at this point that I started to cry. I had hoped to get further along, but it is inevitable. When you open your heart completely and speak the truth from your very being it is a natural occurrence.

I was able to honor Lilly and repeat all of the blessings she has brought to us and keep totally upbeat in spite of my tears. Then I asked Sharon to speak.

She sat beside her and told everyone about Lilly when she was a little girl; about their friendship; about their mischief; most of all, she told of how much she loved her. Other women came forward, honoring Lilly again and again. The entire room was a Kleenex ad. It was impossible not to be drawn into the unconditional love that embraced the entire room. It was glorious. It was pure happiness. It was impossible to describe.

When I left, Lilly hugged me for a long time. I knew initially she was searching her friend's eyes for glimpses of how they were reacting to this special celebration for her. But she got caught up in the love that was surrounding her. I thanked her for a beautiful evening. I was in the glow of the evening's love all the way back to Skaneateles.

First thing the next morning, I got a call from Lilly. She told me the phone had not stopped ringing. Her friends were thrilled to be a part of her special evening. They said they loved the blanket ceremony and wanted to keep it in their lives too.

Ah, I thought. It is truly divine. What a wonderful way to spread love.

CHAPTER 4

YOU'RE INVITED TO CARE

There is a spirit that lives within each and every one of us. It is the watcher of our lives. It's holy and it's divine. It is the editor that lives within us as we are writing and creating the book of our lives. The amount of attention that we pay to our spirit and the power that we allow our spirit to have, has a huge impact on our life's story as we live it. We know that this probably is not a new concept. Many of us have known this since the first time we recognized that we were having a conversation with "our self." It was an internal conversation. Eckhart Tolle has simply called it "self." When I was little I asked my mom about it. She said "That's your conscience, honey." Over the years I have realized that I didn't have to name it.

  This spirit observer aids us in making decisions as we create our life story. The decisions sometimes are tough to make. Sometimes we listen to our spirit plead the case for 'doing the right thing'. And, yes, we know what the right thing is. We know that there is a choice we can make that is loving, truthful, and respectful of God's creations. But sometimes we cave into our inner weakness. We ignore the pleas of our internal spirit. But we know it's always our choice to make. Ultimately we are in charge of our life. The credit or blame that results from our decisions are ours alone. We are responsible for whatever we do. We create a page of life every twenty-four hours. Every chapter is a collection of experiences that contribute to our character and help formulate what we value. Our book is full of wise decisions and our darker side, the human self-seeker who wants to wallow in discontent and egocentricity.

It is the purpose of this book to help you collect some new tools that will add to the magnificence of a celebration of love and new tradition with your families and friends. These celebrations will benefit all who participate in recognizing the divinity of everyone who shares this earth with us. We all play significant parts in this beautiful drama called life. Our intent is to provide you with ideas that you can recreate in your life to make the people whom you love have a richer understanding of how much their life means to you, to those they meet, and to themselves. It is also our purpose to communicate the divinity in those we honor; comfort those in need of extraordinary love and compassion. The intention of this book is to create awareness of the importance of each and every being present in this world. It is also the intention of this book to create in each person the ability to recognize the divinity that God has created in every one of us. We wish to create a river of love that will never stop flowing from your hearts and ours; just think of the possibilities for humankind!

How often do we use the phrase "How are you?" It has become so common in everyday speech that we actually don't even expect an answer. Why? Because it's more colloquial than sincere in its meaning.

Did you ever wonder when this phrase got a foothold in our society? Can you imagine a time when people asked the question and really begged an answer? We are suggesting that the time is ripe for revival of this lost practice of commitment to a potential conversation regarding the well being of another soul who occupies the universe with us. Can you imagine the impact of a sincere inquiry? Would you sincerely welcome the potential answer? Think of the communication that could actually take place. What is the potential in relationship with this shift of intent in an otherwise innocuous question? We suggest that it could be life changing – for you both! Further, we suggest that you not only ask the question sincerely, but you seek out those who seem to desire such a conversation.

Most of us go along without really paying attention to the emotional state of the person with whom we are interacting. We do know when a person is having a bad day, though. It's easy to spot. We see it on the face. Faces are the mirrors of our happiness levels. Before gauging the time commitment you might have to have, we suggest you go forth with full abandon, regardless of time, and show concern for your fellow man.

I am reminded of a time a couple of years ago when my husband and I were visiting friends in Connecticut. My husband had a cold and was not feeling at the top of his game. We were joining another couple for a weekend of golf. They were dear friends with whom we had made many fond memories. Betty greeted us when we pulled into their driveway. She said, as we all do, "Hey, Ed. How are you?" Ed, not giving a typical reply said, "Well, Betty, actually, now that you mention it, I'm not feeling really well." Betty looked at him and said, "Oh, brother! She glanced at her watch and said, "What's the matter?" Ed just looked at her and said, "Well, I've got a cold and I've had better days." Betty replied, "Well, I hope you're not going to tell everybody that asks 'how are you' this story because it's going to be a drag!" We all laughed because, of course, Betty was just kidding Ed. But we all recognized that there was partial truth in what she was saying because, frankly, most people don't want to know how you really are when they say, "How are you?" Betty looked at her watch again, "Ed, you have five minutes to tell me all of your trouble and at the end of five minutes your time is up and you can't tell me any more about how you feel. You are to put on a smile and behave yourself. No more complaining." We all laughed but Ed took her up on the five minutes! He sat down and told her how he had first gotten the cold, and that he was kind of head achy and he was glad he didn't have a fever, but he was worrying about how he might get sicker as the day went on. It was very funny but he used his full five minutes. Betty, looked Ed in the eye and said, "Okay, its over." We laughed and went to the clubhouse to change into our golf shoes.

It wasn't five minutes before another person went by and recognized Ed from past events we had been to at this club. He said, "Gee, Ed, long time no see. How are you?" Ed looked at Betty and Betty shook her finger at him. He looked at him and smiled and said "Oh I'm great, how are you?" "Oh, I'm great too," he smiled as he headed for the locker room.

Most of us do not want to bare our soul to people. It isn't even that we need to do that, but there are occasions when we are hurting   inside. We really want to share that sorrow, but feel isolated because we don't typically do that in our society. It doesn't even have to be sorrow! There are times when we are so joyful that we want to shout from the roof tops. 'Joyful' is the emotion that seems to be shared more easily. We don't want to show our soft underbelly to the world. We like to present the happy face to convince the outside world of our contentment. Most of us try to be positive in our everyday life which is certainly not a bad thing. Sometimes, though, that is tough to pull off.

Wouldn't it be interesting to begin today looking seriously into the face of the first person you encounter and say, "Hey, how are you?" and really mean it? Are you willing to take the risk? Are you willing to give up the time that it may require to respond to the situation that may arise? Are you willing to connect on this highly personal level with someone?

The biggest risk in life that we take is to be open and honest with people. As we mature, we are able to expose our true identity. It is a fantastic experience revealing the 'authentic' you! We so often evolve into anonymity in many of our relationships and never take the additional steps necessary to make authenticity happen. We isolate ourselves. We forget that we are the divine beings that God created to be in this world, with purpose and love in our hearts. We get caught up in the materialism that is dished to us 24 hours a day. We get caught in the whirlpool of life that takes us away from our spirit. We get in the circle of ego satisfying, pleasure seeking pursuits. We forget what it is that we are here to do; we forget our purpose.

Please look at your hands. Look at the left hand and notice the way that the lines are drawn by our Creator. Then look at your right hand. The lines are usually different.

A spiritual woman once told me that the left hand is drawn with promises made to our Creator. The promises we made about the life that we would lead on this earth; the decisions we would make; the road we would follow from the beginning. On the right hand is the life we have led. Most of us see that the choices we have made created some differences. It's then that we recognize why we place one palm to the other as we pray to God. It is our prayer position that we use to match our intentions (left hand) with our actions (right hand) so that life will be lived to the fullest, with the love that is in our hearts.

Ask yourself, "How am I doing, really?" Am I forgetting the important things in life? Am I so caught up in my material life that I am not functioning as a divine being? I remember vividly how out of control I was one day many, many years ago when I was very busy as a professor at a Jesuit college. It was late in the afternoon and I was correcting student term papers. It was getting towards the holiday times and all of the hectic activities that could possibly accompany holiday times were heavy on my shoulders. My children were already home from school, not that they needed me for supervision, but I knew that there were organized sports to take them to, and they had to be fed before all of that happened. Naturally I had nothing in the refrigerator as so many working mothers understand, so I made a quick stop at the grocery store to grab an easy-to-fix meal. The lines were long with similar storied people who were rushing with their own reasons to rush. It hadn't taken too long to find the essentials I was looking for and I noticed an elderly lady heading for a newly opened checkout line. She was leaning against the counter and I thought I could beat her into the line. I felt it wouldn't be a big deal and, surely, she wouldn't have to run around town all evening like I did.

Here's the shame. The woman didn't say a word. She had turned around to see where her husband was and smiled at me. I didn't want to meet her eyes for I was very embarrassed for maneuvering in front of her. But it was so important to me at that moment that I was willing to feel shame. As I was paying for my groceries, I noticed the husband had arrived. He had gently handed her the walker he had retrieved from the car. You see, she was too tired to get out of the store without it and I had made matters worse by darting in front of her. I will never forget that moment. She became one of the most valuable people in my life because she taught me a lesson I will never forget. No matter how inconsequential it seems at the time, never believe your needs are more important than anyone else's. You must always do the right thing. Even if it's not convenient and even if you don't know the other person involved. They are still divine. We have part of their DNA. We share this world with all God's creatures. We do not have the right to over-power just because we are stronger. We don't have the right to assume that our time and our lives are more important then those we disregard, for it is in those dark decisions that our values are lost, and the truth of our purpose is denied.

Your spirit, placed in you before your creation, was placed there on behalf of humanity. You are to recognize your divinity and that of all others who share our earth. It argues first for the best outcome for others, and then for the best solutions for you. The process of this continuous struggle is always there. But you may not be as sensitive to the existence of this priority.

Our actions have a consequence. When we are children, we want to live the lives of our heroes. We want to save the world with our generosity and our kindness. Wouldn't it be miraculous to uphold those dreams?

Unfortunately we are imperfect and sometimes impetuous, giving into our frailties. We make less noble choices. As we get older, we often wonder what our lives would have been like if we had made different decisions. Sometimes the choices we have made have had very unexpected consequences. Perhaps we wish things were different for us.

If you acknowledge that you have, in fact, ignored your greater potential, let's think about it. How can we make a change? Could you be a risk taker? Can you dig into your bag of goodies, the treasures that God gave you for your talent bank, and share your gifts completely, unconditionally, with everyone in your life? Think of the incredible impact that you could have. Remember, life is not about empowering us only for personal gain. It is about using our power to help others as well.

We want you to take the veil from your soul. We know you have this potential because you are reading this book. You have arrived at a point in your life where you understand you have a purpose. The suggestions in this book for spreading your love are made with the best intentions. These ideas are meant to be shared and appreciated with those you love. We hope that you can experience the joy that these creative suggestions offer to you and you will know and recognize the love that you have to share in your life.

Once you have begun these changes, do your own inventory of how you are. Recognize and review your shortcomings and forgive yourself. Acknowledge that you are human, but promise yourself that you will do everything possible to be more: more to the people whom you will see and interact with every day; more to your family; more to your friends. Become the giver not the taker. Feel the wonderful beauty of how it is to live a life that's conscious. Acknowledge the beauty in others rather than yourself. Your spirit will blossom. We promise. Take the risk. The returns are in your left hand.

CHAPTER 5

NURTURING THE HEART

I recently went to Hawaii and returned with a gift for a very good friend of mine who lives around twenty miles away from me. I had been trying to get in touch with Bethany for nearly two months after my trip and we just never connected with a date to meet. Finally, I got to the point that I decided to heck with it, I was just going to show up at her home. I didn't need to stay long but I did miss seeing her and wondered what was happening in her life.

When I was fifteen miles into the trip I telephoned to make sure she was there. Bethany answered and sounded quite tired and probably didn't want company. I told her that I knew I was bad but I said, "Too bad, I'm coming over any way and I need directions." I had tried to find her place before and, although I was in the general area, I never was certain which home it was. When I got there she was in her pajamas and looked exhausted.

I was glad I had the gift from Hawaii because I was

feeling guilty. We hugged and I gave her the present. It was a handmade item that had a story about friendship on the lid. Her husband left us so we could reconnect. Our relationship was built on spirituality. I held her hand as we sat on her sofa, just chit-chatting as women do. During our short visit I told her of the positive thinking I had been working on and that I had some suggestions for material that might help her with the stress in her life. She seemed very receptive, and I knew I would get back to her with help.

It was time for me to leave since I didn't want to drive when the deer begin to wander at dusk. It made driving more dangerous. I explained to Bethany that I had to stop at my sister Vanessa's home on my way back. She lives just five minutes from Bethany so I was killing two birds with one stone. I wanted to deliver a flyer for our 2008 family reunion since my sister's, Vanessa and Sandy and I were coordinating the party.

Bethany and her husband hugged me as I was leaving and I knew I needed to visit with my friend much more often. I was more tired than I thought when I got in the car. Maybe I should just go home and skip stopping at Vanessa's.

I pulled into my sister's yard and was glad to see that my niece's car was there, but unfortunately not Vanessa's. At least someone was there, I thought. The very moment that

I opened the door, I knew I was walking into a bad situation, but I had no idea what was going on.

My beautiful niece, Cindy, is 25 years old. She was standing in the kitchen saying some very odd things between her sobs. I walked over to the living room to check on her two year old daughter, Jean, who had a bottle sticking out of her mouth as she sat anxiously on the couch. Her eyes were fretful when she looked at me. She opened her arms wide, wanting me to pick her up. I told her to come to me because there was a doorway gate preventing me from going to her. She jumped down and made her way to my arms. I held her closely. This child was never around me enough to trust me, but here she was seeking me out. Instinctively, you know when a child is worried or scared, hurt or sick, happy or sad. There was no doubt that this child was worried for her mother.

Cindy had just split up with Jean's father. She clearly was feeling rejected and very upset. I talked to her, knowing that I was not leaving her until my sister returned. It was past dark, around nine o'clock, when Vanessa pulled into the yard. She was relieved that I was there with her daughter. This was a stressful time for Cindy and she couldn't handle motherhood right now. I stayed on in spite of my sister's arrival.

My niece listened as I tried to comfort her. I told her she chose our family to live with, spiritually speaking, and that

I wanted her to know that I was there for her. She had a huge family to draw strength from and we were all there for her.

Between her sobs, I listened to her talk of the struggles and heartache she was going through. I found myself holding her hand as I had just done with my friend, Bethany, not an hour ago. My heart felt her anguish. I invited her to sit closer to me so that could put my arms around her shoulders. I put her head on my chest so that I could hold her even closer. She was in such a fragile state. I rocked her back and forth as I sang my grandmother's old native lullaby.

Our conversation continued as she calmed down. I discovered she was a home-health aide and recently helped an elderly woman on her spiritual journey from this earth. My niece is able to see the 'energy lights' around people. It is an incredible gift for her and for all those she can help. She told me of how she recognized that her patient was moments from death. The lights descended and gathered the woman's energy, ascending just as they had come down. "How amazing you are! I don't see those things! How happy I am for you." I said with great admiration. "You have the strength to help someone through the process of leaving this physical world." Cindy smiled as she blew her nose. I noticed how, with every positive word, my niece sat taller in her seat. We continued to talk.

I suggested that she start writing all of the negative things that she wanted to say to her ex-boyfriend just to get it out. Journaling would be a way to release all her anger and sadness. When she was finished, she could do whatever she wanted with those pages. Burn them, stab them, cut it, tear it, drown it, do a farewell ceremony with it; just do it. Then, after you've put your daughter down for a nap, sit and start writing new pages. Pages full of positives; of your goals. Perhaps plans for tomorrow, then next week, next month, then where you want to be a year from now.

I looked her in the eyes and said with all my heart, "I love you. What would this world be without you? Your beautiful daughter chose you as her mother, and you have to know that. Children are gifts to us and we must protect them and make them feel secure. I know you are capable of this and that you are a strong person. It's a stressful moment in your life, but our family is not going to let go of you. We need you. What would our life be like if you were not in it? We need each other. Let us love you. Let us be there for you."

Cindy promised that she would start as soon as possible with the journaling and thanked me profusely, professing her love for me. I said, "There is no need for thanks, we are family."

Tears were running down my cheeks as I prepared to leave. My sister didn't say too much, even though it was obvious that she had been going through these episodes for some time. I told Vanessa the same thing; that we are family, I love her and we are here to help when she asks. She sighed with much relief and couldn't thank me enough. She called me an angel. Imagine that! I am far from being an angel but I do believe in the power of love.

I drove on the dark country road that night, feeling quite differently from when I started out from my home. I couldn't get over how that little girl, Jean, had seemed to be waiting for me. I knew the flyer I was to deliver could have waited and that I could have done it at another time, but what changed my mind? Had that baby sent me vibes for help? Yes, to this day, I believe that she did.

Cindy was still on my mind. What could I do for her to make her heart happy? The only thing I could think of was the Moontime ceremony. Could I do something similar for Cindy? Why not? I heard my now deceased husband's voice in my head saying, "Val, if it is positive, just do it."

It was so exciting to have a tool to use that would bring compassion and love to someone. I knew it would work. I was a little short on cash so what would I do for a blanket? I decided not to worry about that now. I had to call someone; it was too late to call my sister, Sandy so I called my daughter, Lori. She had not heard the news of Cindy's split. Lori was willing to be there for her.

Bright and early the next day, I talked to Sandy. When I told her of Cindy and what I wanted to do, she was all for it. Now I had to call Vanessa and ask permission, knowing she should have been the first call, but I didn't forget. (Thank you, brother, Jerome, for your necessary advice.) I called my mother, who lives three hours north and she assured me that she would pass the news to my other sister, Nancy and her five daughters. They live in the same area as my mother, Akwesasne, in upstate New York. My mother would make sure they would be there.

My Aunt Tillie was also invited. She lives near me, and I have come to enjoy her company. I respect her. She's had many tribulations in her life and she has weathered them through her 65 years. She continues to be an inspiration to me, knowing the strength and courage she showed after the loss of three of her six sons. I love her. She was delighted to be invited to my 'gathering.'

On one of my sleep-deprived nights before this event, I had the idea to ask my friend, Bethany, if she would like to attend. When I got in touch with her, she was absolutely thrilled to be included in our family event. I knew Bethany would have good words to contribute, even though she didn't know my niece. I wasn't testing or experimenting. I knew she needed to be with us at this time.

I reminded everyone to bring love, strength, and personal advice on the coming Sunday morning.

Now that the time was set, I had so much to think about. What were my words going to be? How was I going to start this whole ceremony? How would I finish? I trusted that my spirit guides would show me by giving me a dream or meditation. I didn't know how to meditate formally, but I know I've been meditating for years. I had so much to say but I never wrote it down. I thought of how I would gather everyone in my kitchen and living room, which is a large area that merges together. That is where I will get them all prepared for this 'gathering' for Cindy.

Tea!

Yes, it would be tea, a special tea. I went to the health food store and asked the advice of one of the helpers. She was in her early twenties, I thought, probably going to college. I remember looking at her nose ring sticking from her left nostril and wondered how does that stay in there? I told the clerk of my nieces' dilemma and my intentions. She was more than helpful with my search. She chose several types of tea, as she talked to herself, moving back and forth down the aisle. Her black spandex top matched her flared capris, intensifying her pale skin. I thought she needed to get out in the sun more. Finally, she chose a tea that proved to be perfect. Tulsi Tea. I will always be appreciative for her being the right person at the right time; a person sensitive to my situation.

During the week, Aunt Tillie, Lori and I went to one of the local Christmas Tree Shops to look for a quilt with a reasonable price tag. Such an adventure it was finding the one that 'feels' right. I was in luck. Actually, I found two; one for my niece and one for her mother, whom I believed was in need of some love-replenishing herself. "There goes the budget," I thought. Oh well.

I was relieved to see my mother come through the door the day before the ceremony. 'Grandma' is always a plus. She had lots of questions and concerns, but let me know that this was her first invitation of this nature and she was honored to be included. My mother is the force of my family, whether she knows it or not.

Sunday morning arrived and I was so tired from lack of sleep. My mind kept going over the things I wanted to say to Cindy; what I was going to do first; what were the words I would use to get everyone into the moment? Would everyone show up?

I gathered my Sacred Indian Tobacco and stood before the cedar tree to pray. I had done the same thing for Karen's Moontime ceremony. I placed the tobacco that I kept in my white deerskin pouch, holding it in reverence as I prayed, putting forth my intentions for my niece. I told the tree why I needed to use its healing branches and I gave thanks for still being here on this earth doing its duty for mankind. I meant every word.

I suppose I could have gone more 'native' with these ceremonies, but I decided it's better if things are kept simple. I brought the branches in and gently rinsed them before placing them into a large stainless steel bowl. I covered the bowl with a dishtowel and set it aside until everyone arrived.

I knew Jill would be tired from traveling abroad, but I called to invite her anyway. She was on her way to church and couldn't make it, but she sent her love and best wishes. She was truly sorry not to be a part of the celebration.

My Aunt Tillie brought some nice cookies to munch on while people trickled in. Mom and Auntie served the tea. Two of my three sisters, Sandy and Vanessa, arrived with their daughters. I introduced Bethany to everyone. They knew she was my friend and made her feel welcomed. She fit in nicely. When my daughter Lori arrived, I quietly took her aside to discuss how better to start out the proceedings. I was nervous but calm, how can that be? I don't know how many deep breaths I took that day, but I filled myself with as much confidence as I could.

Before the ceremony, the phone rang and it was Jill. She was calling from church and seemed quite happy. She told me that while she was praying for Cindy she received a spiritual message. She said that what we were doing for my niece was a positive action but it was like a band aid. Necessary, but she needs to take care of herself after this ceremony and get the help she needs. We are doing our job as a family to uplift her and give her the strength necessary to get the help she needs. Jill said other things too, but I will always be thankful for her love. Jill had a religious experience she will never forget and it was helpful advice when I told my niece of this.

The last group of nieces arrived and it was time to gather everyone in the kitchen. I offered the special tea to bring us all together; it would help us to gather our thoughts for Cindy, who was having some major struggles in her life. I told them of how I was drawn to the house by her little daughter, Jean, (who has some special gifts of her own, I think.) I told them about Cindy's gift of seeing the 'spirit lights'. I explained there was no wrong way of doing this ceremony, so don't hold back from participating. I asked them to use only positive words of truth; that I had cedar water, with the intent that, while using the washcloth, it would be a special time to talk. They were symbolically washing away her troubles, the tears, and her sadness. We were here to give our words and love to Cindy. All were agreeable; what strength I could feel in these women.

My daughter placed a wooden chair in the front of the living room facing everyone. I put the cedar water with the white wash cloth on a small table next to Cindy. I took another deep breath of courage; we were ready.

My daughter started out as planned, showing the others how

it was done for Karen. She thanked everyone for being there as she spoke in a confident tone. She gently started with Cindy's hair, washing off all of her troubles and replacing it with love. It was an intimate sharing with those present. All had tears at this happening; everyone was in the moment. Each had a different relationship with Cindy so the words were different, but all were meaningful and loving for her. I was proud of each woman that had the courage to give Cindy their love and support.

Sandy and her daughter, Susan, were such a big contribution. They were so happy to show their love and affection. I knew in my heart they were always there for any of us. Whenever I call for picnics or any family event, you can count on them. That's what it is all about, I believe. When we are needed; when we are called, we are obligated to go; we are family.

My Auntie is a small but powerful person with such good advice. She was so nervous with Cindy that she even washed between her toes! I laughed as I asked my Aunt to please get off her knees. I told everyone, "Auntie loves to clean you know." She giggled to everyone, "Yes, I do love to clean." It was a tremendous relief to have humor at such a serious moment. Thank you, Auntie.

When it was my mother's turn, she slowly got up from the sofa and rinsed the washcloth thoroughly. I watched as my mother's trembling hands put the cloth to Cindy's forehead. She couldn't help but breakdown as she grabbed her granddaughter's face and said, "I am not letting you go, you are staying here. You are my granddaughter, and I love you." My mother was sobbing as she bent forward to kiss her.

That was it! Everyone began reaching for tissues that I had strategically placed earlier. It was clear to me that it was only a matter of time before they were needed at these ceremonies.

It was Vanessa's turn to talk to her daughter. She was so nervous that she seemed to rush things, but her words were from the heart. She had memories that were shared with us; intimate memories of her love. Her loving eyes told it all as she tried to wash her daughters' burdens into the sacred water.

Cindy's sister, Marnie, knew exactly what she wanted to say and had no trouble expressing it. She was confident and spoke honestly. It was obvious how much the two sisters loved each other, but Marnie was truly concerned for Cindy. We were all touched.

My nieces, every one of them, made me very proud that day as well. They love their cousin and offered emotional support along with their memories of time spent together. They too were moved by being in the moment. Their words were simple as they gave comfort to Cindy and renewed vows of keeping better in touch with one another.

It must have been hard for Bethany to sit and watch all of my family go through this emotional happening. I saw her take a deep breath and step up to Cindy to say the words she had been thinking about. By now, most of the words had been said and it was difficult to think of anything we might have left out. She was slow and very deliberate as she grabbed the washcloth, wringing it out as she began talking to my niece. She talked of how lucky Cindy was to have such a wonderful family who cared enough to gather on her behalf. She talked of how things have a way of working out but it will take an effort on her part, as well as time to heal. My friend lifted Cindy's long hair and began gently washing her upper back. She explained that she knows that's where most of us carry our heaviness, our baggage, and our burdens. My friend was so tender and caring. She really made a difference that day. She shined. Thank you, dear friend.

Finally, it was my turn. Don't you know that I went blank! Well, almost. I reminded my niece again that she chose us as her family, and I hoped after today she would realize just how much we loved her. I reminded her not only of her gifts, but those of her daughter. She needed to help her evolve; without fear or compromise; to realize her capabilities. I reminded her that perhaps she would be called upon to help another family member and I hoped, no, I knew she would step up to the task. I talked of her journaling as a kind of therapy and hoped she would continue with it. I thanked her for letting us come together to help her. I also reminded her that this was just a band-aid, as Jill was instructed, and she needed to work on herself and gain more confidence. I put her on a task of helping with the family reunion, asking her to organize activities for toddlers, since I don't know what a two year old or small child might want to do. I asked her to please stay positive every day. To search for inspirational material, something that would help her find answers to her problems. Then I grabbed the quilt and wrapped it around her, snuggling her inside like a baby. I invited everyone to come up and put their love and strength into the quilt. I told Cindy that when she needs us, all she has to do is wrap herself in our love. I also grabbed the second quilt and wrapped my sister Vanessa in it with all of her surprise. I told her that I loved her and that I knew that she had been dealing with these issues for a while. I hoped it would be helpful to her too. She was clearly caught off guard, but very grateful. Everyone hugged her with love as well.

It was over.

We all sighed with relief and began talking all at once. We were all tired. My mother had made some meat sauce and now it was time for me to put the water on for the spaghetti. Sandy brought a refreshing drink of strawberries and lemonade. It was wonderful to have everyone in this loving mood.

As I was at the stove, one of my nieces from up North, asked me, "Auntie, do you think we could do a ceremony for my sister, Nicole today too? We want to talk to her but we don't know how." My first reaction was, "But your mother isn't here! How can I get her permission?"

She pleaded, "I know, but everyone else is here and we think this would be good for her." It didn't take a lot of reflection. I agreed.

CHAPTER 6

A HEARTFELT GIFT

My niece, Nicole had waited longer than most native girls to have children. Her oldest is a healthy boy, Ross, and soon after his first birthday, Nicole also gave birth to a preemie boy named Wyatt. He had his struggles but did well at a hospital that is well known for its premature birth center. As a family, we all prayed. As natives, we still have our spiritual healers. My brother, Jerome, the Medicine Man, and my nephew, Ben, his apprentice, were ready to provide help for spiritual and medical purposes. There is always a protocol to be followed. Natives have great respect for these people that have learned and kept our ways of life.

Six months later, we were all caught off guard when Nicole's Dad phoned to say she was in the intensive care unit, along with her third baby that arrived prematurely. I remember feeling so afraid for them. I called family members and told them of the situation; everyone was scared but committed to prayers of well being.

Unfortunately, the baby had only the strength to fight for six days.

They buried him on his father's land in Akwesasne, near the   Canadian border. It was such a loss for us all, and Nicole seemed to be in shock or denial, I don't know which. It didn't matter. All we knew was she needed our support. We are just family trying to help family with love and the sharing of our strength. Here we were, having just gone through a beautiful experience for Cindy, and now we were preparing again for a different soul and a different grief. I took a deep breath and knew we could do this.

Nicole's sisters quickly passed the word to everyone. They didn't   question why, they just took their chairs back to the same spots in the living room again. My daughter suggested that I get a blanket from my sewing room; I didn't know if I had anything suitable, but looking through all of my fabric, we found the perfect piece of fleece.

Her sisters asked me to have Nicole sit down because they knew she was shy and she might feel awkward. As she walked out of the   bathroom, I reassured her that this was not planned; that we had no intentions of catching her off guard. Her sisters wanted to take this opportunity to help her and they needed to express their feelings. This would be helpful for them as well, in this healing process. Nicole knew that everyone in the room had her best interest at heart. She could do it. I reminded them that there is no right way or wrong way to this ceremony. We had never done two honorees but were proud that all of them would participate in such emotional events. I thanked everyone for sharing their love.

She smiled nervously towards me as she clutched the wooden chair beneath her. I was feeling her anxiety right along with her. I love Nicole; she is my sister's daughter. I have changed her diapers, fed her, and spent countless hours with her when she was a little girl. She is a unique, soft-spoken woman of few words; a truthful piece of sunshine that I have had the pleasure of having in my life. She is physically twenty-seven, but her soul is old. She is a listener and has learned a lot by having that gift.

This time I started the 'washing'. I felt unprepared, even rushed, but still I knew that I could give words of strength and positive thinking. Before the ceremony, I reminded everyone that this was a new happening; that this was new cedar water.

Nicole's sisters were the first to break down the walls that Nicole unknowingly had built around her. They expressed their own grief and sorrow as Nicole listened intently. They had tears running down their cheeks that they didn't wipe away because they were in the 'moment'. They spoke from their hearts and pleaded with Nicole to open up and let them help her. She didn't say anything; she just shook her head up and down with understanding and agreement. She let them love her.

Sandy had wonderful words of encouragement, and reinforced everything said by the family. She was gentle with Nicole and it was clear that she loved her very much. When she said, "You are not alone. Just ask us for help; let us know what is going on." She spoke for us all.

Susan began by talking of seeing her cousins at family gatherings when they were all much younger. She spoke of how everyone was always together for family functions. She continued with telling of happy memories and, to everyone's surprise, Susan dropped to her knees in front of Nicole, sobbing with words we could hardly understand. She wept as she asked, pleadingly, "Why don't we keep in touch now that we have our own children?" She just couldn't understand why things had to change, I guess. I helped Susan from the floor. No one felt uncomfortable. She spoke from her heart.

My mother said little when it was her turn. She tried to wash Nicole's face but broke down in tears with the words "I love you." That said it all. They embraced like no other time in their lives and they felt it to the core. It was marvelous and it was necessary for us all to share at this moment in time just how much each of us means to our mother and grandmother. Mom is from the 'old school' and has learned to hold her tears in no matter what, but this day, she let it go. She was exhausted.

My Aunt Tillie, having lost three grown sons of her own, told of knowing how Nicole felt; that faith, family and time will help her through her loss. She reminded her of how much she is valued, not only by her children, but by our family. Nicole looked at Aunt Tillie in a different way after that. They are now closer because of it.

My friend, Bethany, had wonderful words to share. She hoped Nicole would hear the words of everyone and let them love her and help her. Even now, Nicole and Cindy speak gratefully for having Bethany at our gathering. They remember her by the good words she shared that day.

We were in a moment, for sure. The unconditional love expressed during Nicole's ceremony was life changing. When we see each other now, it is different. We had been awakened by our Creator. We are now closer than before and we openly share what is going on in our lives. I let my family know that I love them; it is expressed freely. As before, I encourage them to stay positive and to be in tune with their spirituality. Some individuals are at different levels of understanding this phenomenon, and I recognize that. It's not because they are older or younger, it's just that they are at a different place in their lives.

The ceremony has been a great addition to our traditions. I remind my family that when called upon, whether it is a ceremony, a family picnic, or a birthday, they are obliged to come. How rich I feel, knowing that if anything should happen, they will be there for me too.

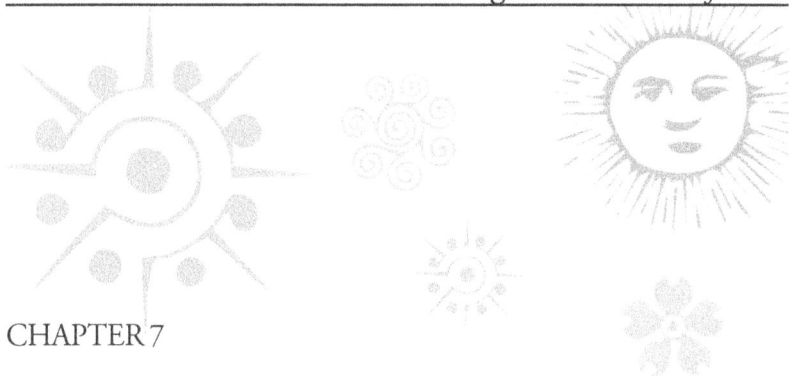

CHAPTER 7

CONNECTING WITH OUR CHILDREN

While writing this book I saw an incredible interview on the Today show (30 Nov. 2007) with Pamela Varady, a Clinical Psychologist, and Sabrina Weill, Editor of MomLogic.com. They were discussing the results of a study regarding sexual activity of teens. They reported that a whopping twenty-two per cent (22%) witnessed sex taking place in school. That's one in five! I had long known there was early sexual promiscuity with young people because of my background in education. But I was dumb-founded at that statistic!

Teens are emotionally pulling away from their parents and turning to their peers in astronomical numbers. They are engaging in adult behaviors, hoping for recognition and acceptance. Many feel abandoned. So, what is missing? What's wrong with this picture?

We embrace our children from the very beginning of their lives. They are the precious centers of our universe. In fact, in some cultures, babies are carried continuously to the age of at least six months; they believe these children are still so close to the Creator that they should not touch the ground. So what happens?

There are many reasons given for the estrangements of children from their parents as they 'grow up'. Parents are too busy working to make enough money to support families; they're living life and not listening; children want to 'express' themselves in their independence. The list could be expanded and it could be very long. The truth is that all of these excuses would not make any difference if an authentic emotional bond existed and continued from the beginning, between parent and child.

Parents are ultimately responsible for establishing a bond of love   between their children and themselves. After all, children are totally dependent from the beginning. They are just receptacles for caring and love. The acceptance of children's divine nature needs to be recognized fully as they continue throughout the relationship with their parents. It is absolutely true that the human side of all of us turns into less than divine actions at times. We forget "We are not human beings having a spiritual experience. We are spiritual beings having a human experience," as Pierre Teilhard De Chardin so aptly put it(in Rosemary Altea's book, A Matter of Life & Death). One of the many challenges on this earth is to remember this when our children are cranky and complaining. In fact, it is difficult to maintain patience for a cranky, complaining adult!

Our main task in life is to reach our children's souls. We need to teach them to value their God given gifts as if they were emeralds. They need to tap into their gifts as soon as they are identified. We then need to teach them self-respect through our admiration. But our admiration must be based on real accomplishments gained by your child, who must constantly use the innate talent given to him or her. These accomplishments include all that is possible through athletic success, emotional maturity and educational acumen. These are the responsibility of the child. This is how they gain genuine self esteem. Adults have to temper their tendency to over-praise children who then get a false sense of ego.

We also have to live as examples for our children in our adult relationships, behaving with integrity and mutual respect. Practicing what we preach. Then we will develop a mature relationship with our children.

Value for our children was so obvious back in colonial times. We had an agricultural society that celebrated every person in the farm community. Most families had several children. Practically speaking, these children would contribute to the welfare and well being of the family unit. They were valued participants in the work of the family. They learned chores on the farm; they had assigned tasks to gather eggs, to milk cows, to help plow the fields and sow the seeds. They gathered crops. In fact, our educational system was designed to accommodate the work of children in the summertime when families needed their help on the farms. Children had incredible importance in our families. They were respected and valued for their contributions.

In the evolution of our society, the scientific and technical aspects of life gradually replaced the agriculture lifestyle. Family units became smaller. We moved from rural communities to the city. Children were now told that they needed to excel in the classroom to get ahead in life. They were told that good grades and perseverance would get them a job where they could earn money to make a good living for themselves and their families. They were told that if in fact they had excellent grades they could go to college and get really big jobs and really big money. The goal for children shifted from that of contributing to the family survival to acquisition of skills needed for future financial gain. They had gone from an obvious, easy- to-understand role in a family to one that is far more abstract.

There seems to be little uniformity in the expectations of children now. Some parents expect children to perform family chores; amounts dependent on their physical capabilities. Some are paid while others are expected to perform without pay because they are living in the family. Some parents have no expectations of responsibilities for their children at all. Different psychologists have different opinions on these matters. It is up to the parents to decide, since they ultimately must prepare children for independence and adulthood.

What is important is that the children feel like contributing members in a family, earning their self worth. They don't acquire self-esteem from doting adults who falsely praise them, knowing no real effort was put forth in any part of their lives: academic, emotional or physical.

As children grow older, we adults often forgive their immature actions by saying,"Oh, they're just teenagers." In fact, in our own way, we often encourage them to be irresponsible and become 'just teenagers'. Are the adults resentful of this or are they pandering to them?

Once out of high school, we hope they are lucky enough to get into a college. We encourage again: study hard, acquire skills. Many are successful. That's what parents pray for.

Continuing with the scenario, let's suppose they are at a working age and many cannot get jobs. We encourage them to gain more experience now, to support the skills acquired in school. Hopefully a job comes along. Some unfortunately may drop out or become discouraged, settling for less than their potential.

The incredible thing about this story, this path of success that we encourage for our divine offspring, is that all we are looking at is the emphasis on the dollar value of their potential worth, post- training. We are looking at their financial future life in the business world.

What happens to the development of their life skills? What have parents and the adult community done to encourage them in understanding the service to others in this life? Is our society's engine totally fueled by financial gain? Is that all we can see as a reward for their talents? Have we commercialized the gratification and acknowledgement in their self-worth? Aren't there other skills to be rewarded? When do they develop their personal sense of identity? When do we tell them about the value they have in our life?

Please don't misunderstand. We need responsible, financially productive people to have a productive society. But I wonder if our emphasis for monetary and material success overwhelms our true purpose. Ignoring our true value can be devastating in the long run. We don't need to look far to see examples of this.

Our schools have added to my concern about the well being of our children as well. Since the centralization of schools, the comfort of small numbers and being known by other students and teachers has disappeared. The reason for centralization is not important in this conversation, but was it a wise decision? I think there were many unexpected consequences. We had to give up so much for our children to do this. They became anonymous in their large, centralized buildings with hundreds of other students. They lost their identity and individuality. People no longer knew them by name. Is there any wonder that finding a peer group has become the focus of their lives? Do you really wonder that many mark their bodies for individuality with tattoos, body piercing and hairstyles? I think we have done our children a disservice in an effort to fix cultural and political problems.

We need to listen to our children. They are crying out and we do not hear them. They need to feel they are valued and loved by the adults in their lives. They need help in developing their nonintellectual talents and abilities. Communities need to encourage safer havens for children in our world. They need heroes in their lives who will be there for them when they are happy, when they are afraid and when they don't understand the way life is treating them.

Those people don't always need to be parents. They can be grandparents, neighbors, or teachers.

Children need consistency in their lives to keep them on their path. They need love, trust, kindness and caring. They need examples that are exemplary. Children need to be taught about the importance of money and the unimportance of money. They need to know about earning money legitimately and what dirty money is: that it comes from prostituting ourselves by compromising our integrity. Children deserve a community that turns its back on immorality.

Integrity seems to be illusive. People seem eager to do whatever it takes to get ahead. That is not what children need to replicate in this life. The term 'earn an honest buck' needs to be modeled and taught to all generations. They need to learn that the acquisition of money is not the chief goal in life. We cannot drag a U-haul behind the hearse.

It's so vital to connect with our children on a personal, loving level. They need to know that you are genuinely in love with them and that you genuinely care about them. It is important that they can rely on you under any circumstance. An authentic relationship is built on a daily step- by- step process of listening, nurturing and appreciating the worth of the child that is in front of you. Observe the pureness of their intent and recognize that they need your help every step of the way. They also need to be able to contribute in every day life, even in an industrial society. They need to find their value through being a working, task completing member in the family by setting the table, or taking out the garbage. They will see that 'work' is not a bad word. Work is what this country has been built with. Work is something we can be proud of.

When children are about seven years old they are able to understand the moral responsibilities of life. They can begin to explore their skills and try to see what path might match these talents as life lies ahead of them. It is never too early to discuss their purpose in life. An easy metaphor is to describe how we are each an important piece of a puzzle. Without our presence there would be a blank space. Life has meaning. They are a valuable contributor to our family on earth.

As children grow and gain life skills, they will understand that we are dependant upon each other. We share our gifts with others for the purpose of helping not only ourselves, but those around us. It is rewarding to help each other along the way. Children can comfort sick or elderly relatives who may need a temporary lift of spirit. A child, when he or she is able to read, has a skill that can be shared almost immediately. They can tutor a younger sibling or read to someone who can't see well.

During my teaching days our college received a grant for a tutoring program to be established in our city's high schools. We recruited 'upper classmen' to teach ninth graders in their schools. It was heartwarming to see how high school students blossomed when they were teaching their younger students after school. They studied harder and honed skills so that they would be effective teachers, able to help 'their' students. These student tutors were remarkable in that they excelled in their own classes as a result of prepping for their jobs. What was incredible, too, is that even though they were offered minimum wages for their time, not one student accepted the money. It was a fantastic testimony to what can happen when children recognize their own talents and share them with others.

So how do we get and keep connected with children? We honor them every single day just as we should honor ourselves and every human being in this world. We need to be demonstrative with children because they need to have our guidance. They need to learn how to conduct their lives in a remarkable way.

We should consider the impact that a Ceremony of Love, previously discussed, could have on the children in our lives. Do they need one? Are you brave enough to try it? You can keep the doors of communication open by entrusting with your child the total truth of how much you love them. Giving them a symbol of that love, like a blanket or a special gift that is extraordinary to them can provide comfort for a lifetime. It doesn't have to be something that is expensive. It has to be something that has meaning between you and that child. It might be as simple as a picture of you both doing something at a special moment in your lives, or a small scrap of a baby quilt that has memories for both of you. These tokens are representations of the love that you have and will always have between each other. They represent the bond that you both carry in your hearts.

I suggest that you make an arrangement with your child that when he or she needs to talk to you and it is very important, they bring out a gift that you shared. It signals to you that you need to listen now, no matter how busy your life may be. If it is really impossible, promise that it will happen within the next hour and certainly before bedtime because that child needs to know that they have an open lane and access to you. They must have that because they depend on you for emotional security and guidance. They need your understanding and compassion when they have problems. The most valuable commodity that a parent has for their child is their time. We may think we are with them a lot, but what is the value and quality of that time? Are you both in the same room but doing different things? Are you driving them to an event when no real communication is possible? Is your time with them spent almost exclusively giving orders, directions and discipline?

As we live our lives in the frantic pace that we have created, it is important to stop and take a deep breath. That breath should fill you with confidence that your true spirit is guiding your life and that you do not have to busy yourself continually with unimportant matters. Make a list of what is really important to you. Make sure that your children are at the top of that list. If you do not have children, be sure you include them in your life through relatives, friends, and neighbors. Children are divine spirits, as are we. They desire and deserve self worth and love. We all do.

CHAPTER 8

BEYOND COMPASSION

It was approximately one month after Cindy and Nicole's gathering when I received a phone call from my Aunt Tillie. It was a Monday evening. She wanted to go to Akwesasne because there had been a tragedy in our family. My first cousin, Thomas, who lives in Oka, Quebec, has a daughter Jessica, who lives in Akwesasne with her husband and little boy. Incredibly, her husband killed their boy and slit Jessica's throat. She had survived through some miracle. It was so hard to comprehend such a vile act.

I picked up my Aunt and I traveled north from Syracuse to my Mom's home in Akwesasne. The wake was to be only one evening, Tuesday, in Akwesasne. The funeral would be the following day farther north in Oka, about two hours away.

The rumors of what actually happened were rampant. The family was trying to find out the truth. Apparently my cousin was going to leave her husband because of his drug habit. They argued. He strangled her and thought he had killed her. When she came to, he ran to the kitchen, got a knife and slit her throat. You would think that would have finished her, but she made it to the neighbor's and they called the police. When they arrived, the husband was standing at the door with the baby in his arms. He had just killed him. To this day I don't know how he did it. But it happened, and the baby is dead.

Before we left for Oka, we found out that the wake wasn't going to take place until Wednesday night, so my Aunt Tillie and I decided to stay overnight. She actually slept at her sister Charlotte's, who was just around the corner from my mother's. I remember I woke up that Wednesday morning, around 7:30 a.m. I went to the bathroom and jumped back in bed. It had been a restless night and as I tried to go back to sleep, I tossed and turned. I kept thinking of Jessica, who was just twenty years old. I knew I had to make a plan. I had to ask Mom and my aunties what they thought first before I could put it into action. I was excited yet I knew how much these happenings can take from your strength. I asked my Mom if she was up to doing a ceremony for Jessica and I knew she would say yes. I told my Mom that I had a problem with using a quilt or blanket for Jessica. It seemed too cumbersome for her at a time like this. So I had my big epiphany, or rather, another thought 'came to me'. I know these things, these ideas, appear to be mine but, they are not. I believe they are from the Creator and all of his helpers. The most natural symbol of love for her would be a shawl. She could wear it at any time without being obvious.

A shawl; of course, perfect. Where could I get one? My Aunt Charlotte would know. I took a shower while my mother called to explain everything to my aunties.

I decided to drive over to Aunt Charlotte's home. On the way I thought of the last time I had seen her. She'd had a near fatal diabetic incident where her kidneys were shutting down. My Aunt Tillie and I went to her bedside in Cornwall, Ontario. When we   arrived, Aunt Charlotte was asleep. We were told she would not live through the day. Her children, all eleven of them, were taking turns on vigil. We greeted each other with hugs and kisses. Aunt Tillie and I looked at each other and knew we were there for one purpose. Every moment was precious and, without talking to each other, started to touch Aunt Charlotte so she would know we were there. We soothed her head, kissed her cheeks, and whispered how much she had meant to us, we rubbed her arms. I whispered 'Thank you for being my Auntie," and she smiled from her closed eyes. Aunt Tillie kept talking to her quietly, saying the things she wanted to say. Aunt Charlotte kept smiling. It was incredible for us to bring her this comfort; she had tears running down her cheeks by this time. I sat near the bed and, while I was holding her, Aunt Charlotte eased out her arm to touch my hand. She held it for the longest time. She then opened her eyes while one of her daughters was whispering to Aunt Tillie regarding her condition and sarcastically said, "I can hear you, you know." Remarkable.

My Aunt Tillie and I had been quite a pair that day, giving my Aunt Charlotte the positive power of love. I don't know how that happens when you just do things instinctively, but that's what we did.

We told her children that they were the medicine of love for their mother; that they had to get over their issues and take care of her. She needed to hear that they will be okay when she isn't here any longer. A lot of her sickness was from stress.

As the hours passed, it was obvious that Aunt Charlotte was gaining her strength. The children couldn't get over how their mother came back to them, just like that. We were there at the right time, I believe, when Aunt Charlotte was deciding to continue to fight or to give into death. We told them that they should take her home since we knew Auntie would like to be there for whatever was to happen.

Now it was one month later when Mom and I walked into Aunt Charlotte's home to talk about Jessica's tragedy. I saw she was sitting in the kitchen, still in a wheel chair. We immediately hovered over her like two mother hens. Aunt Tillie joined in as we touched her from head to toe, kissing her head, her cheeks and her shoulders. How wonderful to experience this level of love. She wallowed in it with much delight and giggled like a young girl.

We knew Aunt Charlotte wasn't strong enough to make the trip for Jessica. She thought she would tire too easily, but she had something for us to give to Jessica. It was the most beautiful shawl, navy blue with long fringe and embroidered flowers at the edges. It was perfect. I couldn't believe it! Aunt Charlotte had one request and that was to deliver a note to Jessica proclaiming her love and support for her. She would feel it in the shawl.

My aunt was on the same page, so to speak. She thought of a way to still help Jessica and knew that it was with love.

So there we were, Mom, Aunt Tillie and I, on our journey with Aunt Charlotte's shawl, not knowing what was ahead of us. As I recall, we did not speak much on our ride to Oka. The latest news was that the baby would not be back from the autopsy in Toronto until later in the day on Wednesday, necessitating the funeral now being on Saturday. Jessica was expected in Oka about an hour after our arrival at her parents' home.

I wondered, "How am I going to ask permission to do our ceremony?" I tried to think of words to say to this young woman. Would she be receptive to this happening? Was she up to this physically? I remember asking again if Mom and Auntie were ready for the emotional commitment; aware that it will be physically demanding as well. Without hesitation they both said yes.

We walked into Jessica's father's home without knocking, as natives do during this time of death. The first person we saw was my cousin, Thomas. He was so happy to see us in this time of great sorrow. He introduced his wife and son. There were other extended family members and friends there as well and I knew they were close because the news of Jessica coming home had just been decided that morning.

I'm telling you there was a whole community in shock over the loss of this little boy. There were counseling appointments set up to help anyone in need deal with the tragedy. The more they talked of him the more they realized that this baby had had a purpose on this earth. This loss made a community step up and address the drug problem that initiated this tragedy. Plans of action continue to this day, perhaps saving God knows how many lives.

Sitting at the large rectangular table were Jessica's parents, my cousin, Thomas, and his wife, Mary. I sat to his left. At the other end was my mother and across was my Aunt Tillie. Thomas wanted to tell us what the real story was to 'stop the rumors,' he said. When he began to speak of that dreadful night, I noticed his wife's reluctance to go through the whole ordeal again.

While he continued telling the gruesome details, I quietly asked Mary for another chair. She brought one back from the porch. I placed it between Thomas and me and asked Mary to sit down near me. Though she seemed to be just going through the motions, she did it without a second thought. I listened to Thomas and, without hesitation, reached for Mary's cold, trembling hand. We sat there as Thomas continued talking of his daughter being attacked and how Jessica's husband stood at the door with his dead baby boy in his arms when the police arrived.

I gently reached for Mary's shoulder and pulled her close to my chest, where I could hold her as she wept. I was a mother comforting another mother over this painful loss. She allowed me to help her. I had to open my heart to this woman. I was becoming more in tune, more spiritual, without fear, doing what I knew I should do. I looked across the room at the other family members and they seemed to be quite taken with the whole moment.

When Thomas finished, everything was quiet. I took the opportunity and asked Thomas and Mary for permission to hold a small ceremony when their daughter came home. I explained that it wouldn't take long. I described how this had evolved from Karen, to Cindy and Nicole and I believed that we could give great comfort and strength to Jessica at a time when it was most needed.

Thomas was honest. "As long as it's not one of those

spiritual things where you're going to talk about the baby and where his spirit has gone and all of that!"

I looked him straight in the eye and assured him, "No, this is about you telling Jessica that you love her, that you are here for her, that no matter what, she has love of family and friends and we are going to share our strength and positive energy right here and now."

He thought for a brief moment as he said, "Perfect. Wonderful, there's no problem." He was relieved. "Want me to get somebody to guard the door so no one disturbs us?" Truthfully, I hadn't thought that far ahead, but I told him it was okay because it was obvious he needed something to do.

I asked Jessica's brother, Tim, to get some cedar branches and not to forget to take the Sacred Tobacco and pray. I assumed that everyone native knew how to set the tobacco at the base of the tree, talking to the cedar of why we need its medicine.

I felt confident, directing in a calm manner; being in the moment. I explained to him what was to be done and he did it without   question. He asked if he could be at the ceremony and I said, "Of course." This was going to be different because the other ceremonies included only women. But why not? This young man needed to connect with his sister and there were no good reasons for him not to be present. It all made sense.

The family called to gather other relatives nearby. It was heart-warming to see how eager everyone was to help Jessica. People awaken with enthusiasm when they realize the need to help is present and they can actually do something to make a difference.

Jessica finally arrived. Her mother explained to Jessica what was going to happen on her behalf and she agreed. We were introduced for the first time and we were comfortable with each other. While she got something to eat before the ceremony, Mom, Auntie and I went onto the porch for some last minute plans and also to collect our thoughts.

I said I would talk to the relatives first to assure them that everyone   was to be of positive thinking and purpose. I reviewed that at the end of the ceremony, the three of us would place the shawl around Jessica, showing and inviting the others to do the same. I asked Aunt Tillie if she would start. She agreed. Mom would be second, demonstrating again the love ceremony that we were to do and the kind of talk we were there to say. She agreed.

We walked back after a few silent moments; I put a chair in front,   facing the couch and recliner. Everyone saw what I was doing. They each found a seat, completing the semi-circle. I held onto Mary and kept her near me until things settled down. We began.

Again, for the people that had come later, I explained how this ceremony originally started. Our purpose for this gathering was to love and comfort Jessica, reminding them of the positive thinking and strength they must share in her time of need. I thanked them.

Everything was going as planned. Auntie was becoming quite a sage, as was my mother. They spoke to Jessica, telling her everything from the heart, without shame or apologies for crying, and everyone followed suit. My chest heaved with respect.

Jessica's friends were thoughtful and said words that made her taller with strength. They were tender, re-establishing their bond of friendship, as they wiped Jessica down from head to toe with good words and love.

Her brother, Tim, got his sister's attention with words of unwavering love and their never-ending connection, which was especially comforting to Jessica. Her aunties poured their love out to Jessica, continuing to give her strength through family. Of course, we were all crying with such sorrow, but with love, too; the ultimate healing ingredient.

I asked my aunt to quietly help my cousin, Patricia, who was clearly going to collapse. (Patricia was actually one of the first people at the scene and if she'd had a weapon....well, I don't want to even imagine.) My aunt was soothing Patricia without making a scene, while I mentally asked my cousin to look at me. I insisted. She took deep breaths as my aunt talked into her ear, stroking her hair for consolation. Patricia looked at me. I told her with my eyes that everything was going to be all right and that she was a strong woman, that her niece needed her. I calmly lowered my lids and smiled as my cousin retrieved her composure. I took a deep breath as the person talking to Jessica was just leaving her side.

Mary appeared to be fragile but when it was her turn to address her daughter, she became the most inspirational person of all. Her connection to her daughter was renewed again that day, because they had grown apart, though they were only two hours apart. Mary told Jessica to come back home with her family, even if it was just to recover from this emptiness and loss. She held her daughter's face and made it clear how much Jessica is loved and that she and her   father will always be there to help, no matter what. They held each other so long and tenderly, rocking back and forth in each other's arms.

My cousin, Thomas, had gone to rest before the ceremony and couldn't be awakened. He hadn't slept for two days and nights, waiting until his daughter came home. He chose to release his anger and accepted the Creator's plans for his grandson. I thought he was a champion by setting an example of keeping his faith. I hoped more of us could be like him.

Then it was my turn. I wish I could have said all the things I had thought of for Jessica, but sometimes less is better. I looked around at the family and friends as I stood up to gather the washcloth. I thanked everyone for their wonderful words of love for Jessica and her son. I apologized to everyone for meeting for the first time like this and that I am to blame for not making the effort during better circumstances. I explained that after I talk to Jessica, my Mom, my aunt and I would have to leave for Akwesasne and then on to Syracuse to keep other obligations. I then turned to Jessica and told her to look at the family that was there and to remember their faces and perhaps in the future, she can help any one of them in a time of stress. I told her most of the positive words had been said but to remember them in the coming days because when she needs help, she will see these faces and they will give her strength. I thanked her for allowing us to help her, reminding her that even if this was our first meeting we would always be family.

I gave her the note as I explained how the shawl came to her and why Aunt Charlotte wanted her to have it. She cried when she read it. I asked her to stand up and placed the shawl around her. Mom, Auntie and I took action silently, kissing her, touching her hair, making sure she was safe within the shawl.

I invited the family and friends to come up and do the same. I told them, "You will be empowering this shawl with your love and strength and in the coming days, when Jessica needs it the most, she will wrap herself with this love and strength, she will wipe the tears from her eyes with this shawl and she will remain comforted in this moment forever." Everyone understood the power of that moment.

It was over.

We were polite and waited briefly, but our mission was over. They offered food and drink for our travel and we were thanked by everyone. I nodded to Mom and Auntie, who were looking at me as well, and we slipped out to travel home. We didn't talk much for quite a few miles but I started by thanking them for their help in the enormous ceremony for Jessica. I told them how proud I was of them and how much they were needed, especially at this ceremony. I reminded them that they each have experiences with loss of children. I do not. I did know the loss of a loving companion, as I had lost my husband the previous year.

I have to say that we felt good by helping someone through the most difficult of all times, and this was certainly it. Jessica was going to need all the strength she was given. I guess it was when I held her hand; when I explained what we intended to do that I felt Jessica's body react to her unbelievable loss. I felt her panic; saw her eyes searching the room for her son so she could leave; saw the realization of her fate. I felt her emptiness that will never surrender to time. So much pain. I am so, so sorry.

It took me a week and a half before I regained my strength, but it was worth it. I would be there for her again if asked.

I have not heard a word on how things are going with Jessica. I am planning a trip to Oka before winter sets in, just a visit to check in with my nieces. Nicole wants to start back to college to become a court reporter. Cindy continues with her job as a home health aide but has told me she is journaling and loves it. I remind her of the 'band aid;' that she needs to seek professional help for some issues if she needs it. I will continue to check on her as I do with most family members.

I quit my job to pursue my spiritual awakenings and I continue to have 'events' going on. It matters little if someone believes the life-changing effects of these ceremonies; heck, sometimes, I have a tough time believing myself. I am acting on these 'events' much more promptly now. I recognize that probably most of my life, I was not listening. I listen now.

I encourage you to not be afraid. How can something positive from the Creator and the light be wrong? Trust in yourself and ask for the things you want. Listen to what is being sent your way. What is the purpose of dreams? Each of us has the opportunity to experience the love and positive energy that we can create for ourselves and others. Draw to you the strength that you want and need. Let me know of your progress from time to time. Be patient; more patient than you believe possible. Be deliberately good to yourself and take the time to replenish your soul and your sunshine. Don't wait for others to make things happen for you; smile and go with the light every day. Be the observer. Comfort and console those in need. Celebrate life. Respect the divinity in all those we meet, wrap them so they may wrap others in the quilts and shawls of spiritual love. Share your energy and love by starting your own ceremonial traditions. Take your positive power and change the world.

Be silent and listen to your heart, be still

Believe and ask the Spirit Beings

For the help you may need

Be thankful for the comfort

Let gratefulness flow

Rejoice in their love

The Spirit Beings, ever present

We are safe

We are loved
Be silent and listen to your heart, be still

Nya wenh' (Thank You)
Val Cook

Sharing the Medicine of Love

CHAPTER 9

PLANNING A CEREMONY

Some of us are lucky enough to have found our purpose in life; some of us are still searching. Those lucky ones have been observant of their gifts and work toward discovering what they need to do on their journey. One thing for sure, no matter where you are on your path, you must realize that we all possess the powerful gift of love.

Our ancestors have passed on other gifts from the light, including wisdom in its many forms. That wisdom is sometimes forgotten through a generation and it escapes us for long periods, giving us difficulty in our lives. Many are of the opinion that now there is an upsurge of energy and love that is coming from the universe, reminding us of the potential power we possess. Scientists have begun to challenge the existence of this spirituality with positive results for those who have been skeptical. It seems that there is a bond between mind and spirit, which spiritualists never doubted. In fact it has been proven through scientific experiments that people who are sick and have been prayed

❄ 83 ❄

for have a better chance of improving than the not- prayed-for group. Knowing this, it is exciting to think of the possibilities that we all have within our grasp.

Val and I invite those who read this book to embrace this power that is always available to us, as individuals or as a group. We invite you to adopt some or all of the ceremonies that we have described. In fact we encourage you to create your own well intended spiritual gatherings. We ask you, too, to embrace the messages given to love one another, especially our children. It will impact you and the whole world with waves of inspiration, compelling you to experience love to the core in your family.

The following are suggestions and recommendations for you to prepare yourself for the ceremonies. First, be cautious about jumping into a 'ceremony'. There is much preparation to ensure that the maximum positive impact will occur for your loved one. Ask yourself some questions. Am I emotionally ready to honor this person? Am I completely open to this gathering? Do I want to do this one to one or should I include certain other people in their life? Which is the best for them? Review mentally how the ceremony would go if you had the perfect situation. Be sure you leave yourself as much time as possible for planning. It is rare that you won't have the luxury of time on your side. Above all, be a good listener and observer during your preparation.

Naturally the type of ceremony will demand different protocol. For instance, if you're celebrating Moontime with a daughter, granddaughter, niece or friend, then it is necessary to obtain the mother's permission. Probably no permission is needed for a birthday celebration.

Sometimes people are experiencing sorrow and loss, or they are having a new experience that is producing anxiety and depression for them. Without being a doctor or certified psychologist we honestly can't offer professional aid. What we can rely on is our life skills. Everyone has the potential to interact in a positive way with their family and with their friends. We have experiences to draw from our relationships. We know that we are able to uplift one's heart when we acknowledge their accomplishments or positive traits. We also know that sometimes we need to simply say "I love you". When it seems like an extra effort is needed to elevate someone, it is time to consider a ceremony.

Keep it positive
Whether you make a decision to honor a life by hosting just the two of you or having a gathering of many, it is important that you keep the ceremony up beat. This is not the time to drudge up the sorrow that created the need in this loved one. We can't question why they are in the life they are in, or why they're living it. We embrace their situation without judgment and only offer our compassion and love. We are here to help them realize they have so

much to offer the world. They need to be reminded of their attributes and the significant role they play in our lives.

Negative thoughts and negative words do not have a place in the celebration. It is not the time to say you are sorry either. A ceremony is reserved for only the person seated in the chair of honor. For those who have a larger gathering, it is important that participants are aware ahead of time that this is their opportunity to pay tribute to the divinity of the celebrant. All of the beautiful traits, all of the beautiful habits, all of the beautiful memories that have been shared between the honoree and the celebrant are the focus of the ceremony.

What are your intentions?
It is extremely important to ask yourself and those attending the gathering, "What are your intentions?" If the intentions are pure and full of love, that will assure you that the ceremony will be a success. The individual you are honoring is worthy and shares the light that brought us all to this earth. You are giving to this person all of the gifts that he or she deserves.

Tokens of love
The third thing you need to consider in preparing for the ceremony is to bring something that is special between you and the honoree as a permanent reminder of the love and gratitude you hold for them. This is in addition to

the quilt or shawl that you have selected. Nobody has to bring an expensive gift. It may just be the words from your heart.

We all have different levels of love and kinds of experiences that we bring to this person. It could be a unique memory, moment, or personal interaction. If you do bring a gift make it significant between you and the receiver. It will personalize that moment and it will always be remembered. Maybe it is a journal. Maybe it is a beaded barrette. Make it special. It's not about showy, material giving. We're talking about giving from your heart something that is very, very special between you and that person.

When there are participants
If your gathering includes more than you and the honoree, then you can have as many people as you think is plausible. It depends on what the purpose may be for honoring that person. If there are many people involved, it is important to tell the invitees ahead of time, if you can, about the planned ceremony. They can come pre-pared with their words, with their small gift, and with their love that will be special between them and the honoree. If you have a gathering that includes only family except for one outsider, be sure to be especially welcoming to that person. They're there because they are someone special to the person being honored, invited just because of that relationship. It is important to embrace

them not as a stranger. It is a way of respecting this person and acknowledging the important part they will play in the ceremony.

Setting
In planning the celebration consider the setting and make sure it is as intimate as possible. You might want to have candles lit in the room. You might want to have incense burning. You might want the chairs situated in a certain way, like a semi - circle or a full circle. You might want to all sit on the floor. You might all be outside on the lawn in the summertime on a beautiful moonlit night.

The setting is important. Remember you are building an incredible memory for this person who is receiving the best of all love from everyone who is participating in the celebration. It is up to you if you feel comfortable 'cleansing' the honoree as part of the ritual. If you choose to include this, be sure to include a wash basin, filled with warm water which is infused with any one of a number of choices: a cedar branch, rosemary, rose petals, lavender; the list of possibilities is endless. What scent does your celebrant enjoy?

If you choose not to use water, you may wish to include a special scent in the room by burning candles, incense or spraying a special fragrance into the room.

How to begin the ceremony

The facilitator or organizer of the celebration should welcome all of the invitees. Perhaps they would say: "Thank you all for coming to celebrate the life of this beautiful person who will soon be in our presence. Thank you for having a positive frame of mind for keeping only positive thoughts and love for her. Realize that you will always be remembered for having added so much light and love to this person's life. Thank yourself for recognizing how important it was for you to be here and to bring the best side of yourself so you could share tonight."

Place beside the chair [or on the floor] the special blanket or shawl that you will be using for the celebration. Be sure that you turn off all the telephones in your home and ask people to turn off their cell phones so there will be no outside disturbances. Sometimes you might want to have some spiritual or classical music that would be meaningful before or during the gathering. It's wise to keep it on a very low volume so it isn't distracting.

Final preparation

Before you ask the honoree to join you, remind the participants once more: This is the reason we are here: to help our mother through the loss of her sister. [Whatever the purpose]. Thank you for bringing your good words because the positive thinking that will be here today will be uplifting; especially thank you for sharing your love.

Now we're going to gather in the living room: I have cedar water [or whatever it is you're using] and we will begin shortly."

After everyone is seated, you call the person who is being honored into the room. There is no need to applaud or anything. It is a very serious moment; it is a very intense, personal, intimate moment for this individual and you're going to connect with them in a very deep way. If your ceremony includes the use of water and you are the first person to honor the celebrant, take a washcloth and put it in the water, wring it out and kneel down in front of the honoree. 'Dab' their face, if they have makeup [I don't know the age the person you're celebrating]. The purpose of using the water is to keep contact with the honoree with each stroke [not to really wash them]. You touch their face, their hands and their feet. You are there to share the love that you have for that individual. Usually there will be initial awkwardness, but it is all right because there is no pretense in what you are doing. When it is time to wash the person, start touching them first, perhaps putting your arm on their shoulder. You are in the moment with that person. It doesn't matter about anybody else in the room. It is so intimate and important that you are immersed in the relationship with that person at that moment. The little things, thoughts and expressions you bring to her will be remembered forever.

As the organizer, if you choose not to use the water, it is

important that touching of some kind be involved. Use your hand to touch a shoulder, an arm, hair, rub across the eyes. Hold the hand. Embrace with the love that you feel in your heart for them. You may want to use a bough from a fir tree. It depends on what you have in mind. Again, ask yourself what is the intention for this person? You know this person more than most do. You need to be comfortable with them. You have to be comfortable in the way you are honoring them as well.

After everyone has interacted with the honoree, it is important to then have the person who organized the gathering place the shawl or blanket around this individual. This is a symbol to be taken home and have forever. It represents the love and beauty of the moment shared with all of these important people in their life.

If the choice is to use a shawl, make it a longer shawl that feels comforting and substantial and will wrap easily around her. She needs to feel her womaness. Because it is long and luxurious she will feel somehow protected from the world. It may, in fact, be viewed as a protection shawl. It will keep her unexposed and safe from vulnerability. If she is Native there will be prayers and offerings of tobacco to the Creator for that individual's supporters well. If she is a non-Native, the shawl will probably be the only representation of protection she has ever experienced. She will be able to enwrap herself for evermore in that shawl.

The blanket can be equally powerful. When it is placed around the celebrant, be sure that all the loving words that will comfort her are spoken. Tell her that the blanket will always be with her, whether you are with her or not. It may be a nice gesture to ask, if the number is not unruly, to ask all who participated in the ceremony to come forth and hold the shawl around that person and touch them with their love. The blanket is then wrapped around her again so that the impact of all the love that is present will always be in that moment for her forever. It will also be in every one else's memory. The odors you create (like orange, lavender or vanilla) will be instinctively responded to whenever it is experienced in the future. These will be triggers of love for them if you want them to be.

The emotions that are expressed in these gatherings are powerful. It is extremely common for everyone to cry because this is a truthful, beautiful expression of love. If you become anxious during the ceremony, breathe in. Fill yourself with the purity of your intention and the confidence that you know that this is coming from your heart. You are connected with your family and your friendship. This is special and everlasting.

After the ceremony
You might want to follow the celebration by serving tea or something that is appropriate for the participants. Since the honoree is not at the event until you actually begin the celebration, this is a real opportunity for all to gather

together so that everyone can enjoy the moment. Tulsi tea which is a "gathering tea" is not full of caffeine, and is often used by Val. She has everyone sit around the kitchen table and sip their tea, getting caught up in the conversation. It tends to make people a little less uneasy and they can experience the joy of the moment. Everyone can take a deep breath and be happy for being present at such an extraordinary event.

So now you know how wonderful the celebration can be. Be brave enough to start your own traditions. Run with it. Begin your own ceremony. There are good people in your life who are in need of your support and love. It is the time to offer it; love beyond imagination. What good is it to love if you keep it to yourself? Sharing love is the way to eternal happiness. Beginning these ceremonies in your family does not cost a thing. You know in your heart of hearts that you will be sharing a beautiful tradition together. You don't have to be rich or poor. You don't have to do anything exclusionary. It is all positive. There are certain suggestions we have included to help you get started. So go forward. Be the one. Be the light. You'll feel heavenly.

CHAPTER 10

CREATING MALE RITUALS

It almost seems like we need to rebalance the earth, to put pureness of heart back in line with the mind. We need to establish ground rules for living. We need to build respect for self and humanity. The latest statistic is that there is a death every twenty seconds, with male deaths far outnumbering women. What can we do? We need to attempt to rescue our boys and young men from the ravages of society. One possibility is to help educate them in finding their purpose.

Men begin as women do: pure and untainted. Turmoil greets us all, but some are affected more than others. It seems there is a point in maturation when some males become very guarded in communicating from their hearts. Some seem to elaborately cover up their fears; humility is replaced by bravado or machismo in their teen years. It seems that these behaviors stem from a lack of clarification of their role and purpose. The incredible responsibility and expectation of the male as provider appears to be overwhelming at times. Are they trapped in the drudgery of their hearts, with no place to turn?

Many men do not learn to differentiate between family love, romantic love and lust. Some men appear to feel awkward in expressing love to other men or family members. Do they learn, as small children, how to express emotions to family and non-family members? Is their socialization that different from females? They seemed to be conditioned to the ritual of a handshake as the exclusive expression of friendship. Do they fear that a more physical expression of affection could be interpreted as lust? Do they need more training on the types of relationships that exist and the appropriate ways to behave in them? One can only imagine how limited men must feel.

Val and I have given much thought to what can be done for men. We would like to offer the same kind of solace that is offered to women in the ceremonies described in this book. Unfortunately, at this time we can only offer a dream that Val had, along with a discussion of male rites of passage in the Native American society. We will continue to ask for help in this area.

Val's Dream

Although I have grown up with giving 'Thanks' to the Creator nearly every day, I have found myself talking more and asking for more and more. I don't feel shame for asking for too much too often because I love the Creator and he loves me. I have dealt with my husband's death as positively as possible and never once been angry or felt cheated by God. We had found each other in this world and wasted no time falling in love with each other. If love was a disease, we wanted it. If having loved meant heartache, loss and sorrow, we were willing to embrace it. We both loved being in love and felt fortunate and happy.

Now my time is spent with family and good friends. I look back at all my writings of dreams and experiences and find that they have been messages rather than my own ideas.

One of the things I have asked the Universe about is how to help men with their spirituality; how to release any negativity that may be inhibiting their growth and feelings of worth; and how can they learn to express and accept love?

Shortly after seeking the answer, I was awakened with a memory or thought. I saw myself closing a door and seeing that I wore a long beach dress over a bathing suit as I walked towards a manmade waterfall. It was a large room with the water cascading down a four foot waterfall, down to the two steps before the water drifted into a rounded pool. On each side of the waterfall were flowers and vines offset by soothing lights. In the background I heard peaceful music as I approached the man sitting on the second step in the water.

He was of medium height and weighed about 200 pounds; he had on bathing trunks with no shirt. He looked at me with anticipation. I greeted him in a calm manner and asked him if he was ready to begin. He was. I slipped into the water behind him, sitting on the first step with his back to me. I told him that I wanted him to start listening to his breathing; to close his eyes and smile. He did this without question. I pulled him towards me like a child to his mother and caressed him with my legs, his head rested on my chest. He took a deep breath and let it out slowly. I asked him to listen to my voice and to keep smiling; this was most important. I picked up the water and put some on his head. I put more on his forehead, eyes, nose, ears, mouth and shoulders as I explained that each time I brought the water to his body, I was washing away all of the negativity held in these areas. I was washing away the layers of guilt, fear, jealousy, heartache, trauma and any old issues or memories of harm to him or to others. "The water flows in one direction", I said. "Focus on a bright positive future." I symbolically opened his chest and pulled out the hurt and negativity and threw it to the water. I paused and told him to keep breathing.

After a few moments, I took water and placed it on his head and said "This new water is healing your thoughts and you will only have good thoughts from now on." I put water on his forehead and said "This new water is to help you think better about yourself and others. This water will help you to see things in a better and more positive way from now on. This water will help you to hear only positive things and hear more clearly what people are saying to you. This handful of water will help you to smell and taste things in life in a more positive way. It will help you to notice smells and taste things as if it were the first time. You will choose your words more carefully, only saying positive words from positive thoughts. Your shoulders will carry only what you need to carry and you will smile every day because you feel so much lighter. This water I am putting on your arms and hands are to bring only the positive to you and will stop any negativity from coming nearer than arm's length. I have opened your heart to release any negativity. Now it is time to put the sunshine that you were born with back into your life, with all of the dreams and strength to help you with the rest of your life. Know that you are a loved person by our Creator and He will always be with you.

I wiped the tears from his cheeks and we left the waterfall together. I wrapped him in a large towel and held his face in my hands. I thanked him for our time together and I told him that he was a good person and would now be even better as he continued with his positive journey.

The next thing I knew was that this man was giving me lots of money; handfuls of money that spilled onto the concrete tile.

I asked my brother, the Medicine man, Jerome, what he thought of this whole vision. He told me it probably meant that what I gave this man was worth a great deal of his money.

Rites of Passage

What I am about to write are only assumption, ideas of my own, hearsay and family knowledge from my brothers and their own experiences.

I have six brothers and three sisters. Many of them have acquired skills and have been given spiritual 'gifts.' We grew up on the Onondaga Nation, south of Syracuse, in upstate New York. One brother, Jerome that I am particularly proud of has spent most of his life learning herbal and spiritual medicines from elders, far and wide, in the United States. He has not restricted himself in learning, so to him, all things are possible. He has in turn been able to share his knowledge with his brothers and nephews, all of whom are in the 'Wolf'clan. He has brought to our family a very great thing; his knowledge of medicines. He pursued it rigorously and let nothing stop his growth. We ask him, on a regular basis, for spiritual and medical help when it's needed. He remains unassuming in public and I respect him for all that he has accomplished so far in this life.

One of the rituals that he has brought to the males in our

family (and invited males outside of our clan) is the 'Rites of Passage.' This is a foundation for them to continue. It includes four to sixteen years of learning. This training is specifically for those men that have chosen to enter the area of medicine, both spiritual and herbal.

I listen to my brother's conversations regarding the experiences they have when it is time for them to gather each year. I've learned there are many procedures: first, of asking permission for a piece of property with a stream to wash in; a secluded place to build shelters; then, a willingness to bring skills they know; and a desire to learn while working together to build crude shelters. I think the idea is to spend time together, work together, eat together and accomplish more than just building shelters. They know that they must fast for four days with only a prepared drink (containing I don't know what, other than prayers.) Each participant hires a woman to sew a white robe that he will wear   during the four days of fasting. This woman must be beyond her Moontime years and may also be hired to cook for them when they return from their 'rebirth.'

They are taught and reminded at this time of how to conduct   themselves in life. They are given obligations, to stay positive and determined to be the best they can be. Two of my brothers have come from Florida to Syracuse four years in a row to participate in this ritual. They make things happen for themselves. They work together, planning from year to year. Usually the family will gather at this time with gifts, giving support to the men for their   accomplishments. We prepare their favorite foods to celebrate their happiness and provide family support when they emerge from the days of fasting. I remain proud of them all.

Recently, I asked my nephew to help me put together a ceremony for my grandson, who is thirteen and going through puberty. My daughter is a single mother who is doing a great job of raising two children but a boy needs male influence to let him know how he is doing and to give him guidance.

My nephew and I have discussed issues that I would like him to keep in mind, such as using positive power; respecting one's self and others; being thoughtful towards family and community, and practicing charity. My nephew also needs to teach my grandson what is expected of him as a member of a family, clan, community and Nation. He also needs to stay strong in both body and spirit. These are just a few of the many things we have discussed.

For the ceremony, I expect that the men of our family and a few clan relatives would attend. Each would be given the intentions for my grandson so that they may bring wisdom and gifts of encouragement. My mother, my daughter, his sister and I, four generations, will help to prepare a feast in celebration. It will be his day to sit at the head of the table, honoring him with respect, now that he is a young man.

This ceremony could be more elaborate, but this is what I have at this time. Perhaps you can use this as a basis for such a gathering. I think, rather than use the washcloth with the cedar water to symbolically shed the childhood from my grandson, I might suggest a branch of white pine. This could serve the same purpose as the water for my granddaughter's Moontime ceremony, except that the branch will lightly brush away the 'child' from the young man, giving the celebrant an opportunity to talk of the pride he has through giving words of wisdom or offers of teaching him: welcoming him to sit with them from now on. His father, uncles, grandfathers, and any person invited will now talk of how they have watched out for him all of these years and how he must watch over his sister, cousins, and female relatives. They have now opened a line of communication with one another and this will last forever. The female relatives will provide a new blanket, and the person in charge, perhaps my nephew, will place this around him at this time. Others will present their gifts. All will shake hands and hug each other. It will then be time to give thanks to the Creator and to eat.

CHAPTER 11

REFLECTIONS

You are being invited to join our circle of infinite love, hope and harmony. By participating in these ceremonies we hope that there will be a metamorphosis in your life. You will have an internal awakening of your purpose. You will experience an affirmation of self-value and a filling of love that will replace self-doubt.

At one time we knew, at top of mind, that love is the one most important aspect of our being and the one most important gift we must share. This love of ours, given unconditionally by our Creator, is to be shared freely with those around us, not even limiting us to our family and immediate friends. Indeed, we are to spread this incredible soul-nourishing bond of love with those who enter into our world.

This manual is not easily written, nor easily followed. The nature of the human expectation in these ceremonies is profound. Val and I ask you to embrace these we are not doctors or psychologists; we are souls who are simply awakening to our purpose. As you read these experiences we hope you can sense the magnitude of love and commitment that is present. We also hope that you embrace these concepts so that you, too, can spread love in your world. Ultimately we realize that our society desperately needs to share the love in our hearts so it can wash away the insecurities, sorrow, isolation, and fear from those whom we meet in our lives.

All generations are suffering from chaos which is created in our world. Overwhelmed by this insanity, many experience sorrow and despair in our lives, often separating themselves into small islands of discontent. The consequence of our psychological isolation and moral deprivation has created a world full of hate and impersonal response. Many of us live in an enigma; our children are often lost; our lives seem more than we can sometimes bear. Nothing seems to fill our emptiness, not the plasma television, not the shiny new jewelry, nothing. The temporary rush of materialism is soon absorbed and the emptiness returns. We have been sucked into the physical world, sold into the notion that 'stuff' will fill the hole of discontent.

We can all see the folly in our existence. The good news is that we need not look far for the solution to the problem. We can fill our chasm of need. Moses told us the answer, as did Jesus, Confucius, Mohammed and yes, the Beatles. All we need is love. We receive that love through the action of loving. This is how to exist happily in our world.

Kabbalah teaches that we are receptacles of God's love. We need to empty our love into others, hoping to be like our Creator who teaches "Love thy neighbor as thyself." Unfortunately, many of us have forgotten how to do this. Our purpose, then, is to awaken our senses to this phenomenon.

Can you remember the last time someone told you what a thoughtful person you were? Our physical receptors almost swoon at the recognition of self worth! It just feels good. It's like getting a new piece of furniture; but this feels good in our soul. It is this piece of wisdom that so many have forgotten. We want to create a bond of love and connect with everyone who enters our lives. Sometimes you may choose to connect through ceremonies of love.

A higher purpose is at hand. We ask that you embrace it. At birth we are nourished and grow, unimpaired by our biological assignment. But without love our progress is hindered. It is a fact that infants will grow for a time without human touch, but will lose weight and falter in their growth eventually. Without love we cannot survive. For those who have love, growth is limitless. The vast majority of the human race is found between these extremes. We are seeking to emotionally evolve and not be 'stuck'.

Being stuck is not where God intended our evolutionary process to be. He gave us an enormous survival instinct, which many of us have turned inward. We have chosen egoic pursuits. We constantly compare our successes to those of others; we judge before we get judged. We carry chips on our shoulders. Some express who they are through body piercing and body painting. We show the world that we can be self made with or without the love we are constantly craving. We are overachievers, underachievers, body slicers, and drug abusers. We will seek the physical fix we need to replace what is missing in our lives: love.

The ceremonies in this manual cannot change years of separation, disappointment and emptiness, but it's a sensational opportunity to experience unconditional love. Please join in the circle that is one with the Source. Our egos are no longer needed to layer protective mechanisms that just sustain the emptiness that ravages us. Our energy field is fueled by the power of God's love that is ever present.

We are not doctors or psychologists. We are simply following our instincts. We ask you to participate in ceremonies and withdraw from fear of rejection and exposure. Please recognize that supplanting our ego with openness is the only way to rid our false armor of protection, forged from disappointment. A world of sorrow can be transformed into self-acceptance, forgiveness and the bright light of love. It can be possible to live to your potential. You are free to explore your purpose; to live without constraint and self doubt. You will know that failure does not equate with unworthiness. Our development is procured from the pillow of love that carries us into the world we can now create. Our possibilities are limitless. We are empowered by love. This common thread is pulled by one source; pulling the fabric of the quilt and the scarf, each piece unique, into one pattern of existence.

If love is what you see, it will be love that you live.

www.ingramcontent.com/pod-product-compliance
Lightning Source LLC
LaVergne TN
LVHW091156080426
835509LV00006B/716